KU-351-613

Cultural China Series

Lin Ci

CHINESE PAINTING

Capturing the Spirit of Nature with Brushes

Translated by Yan Xinjian & Ni Yanshuo

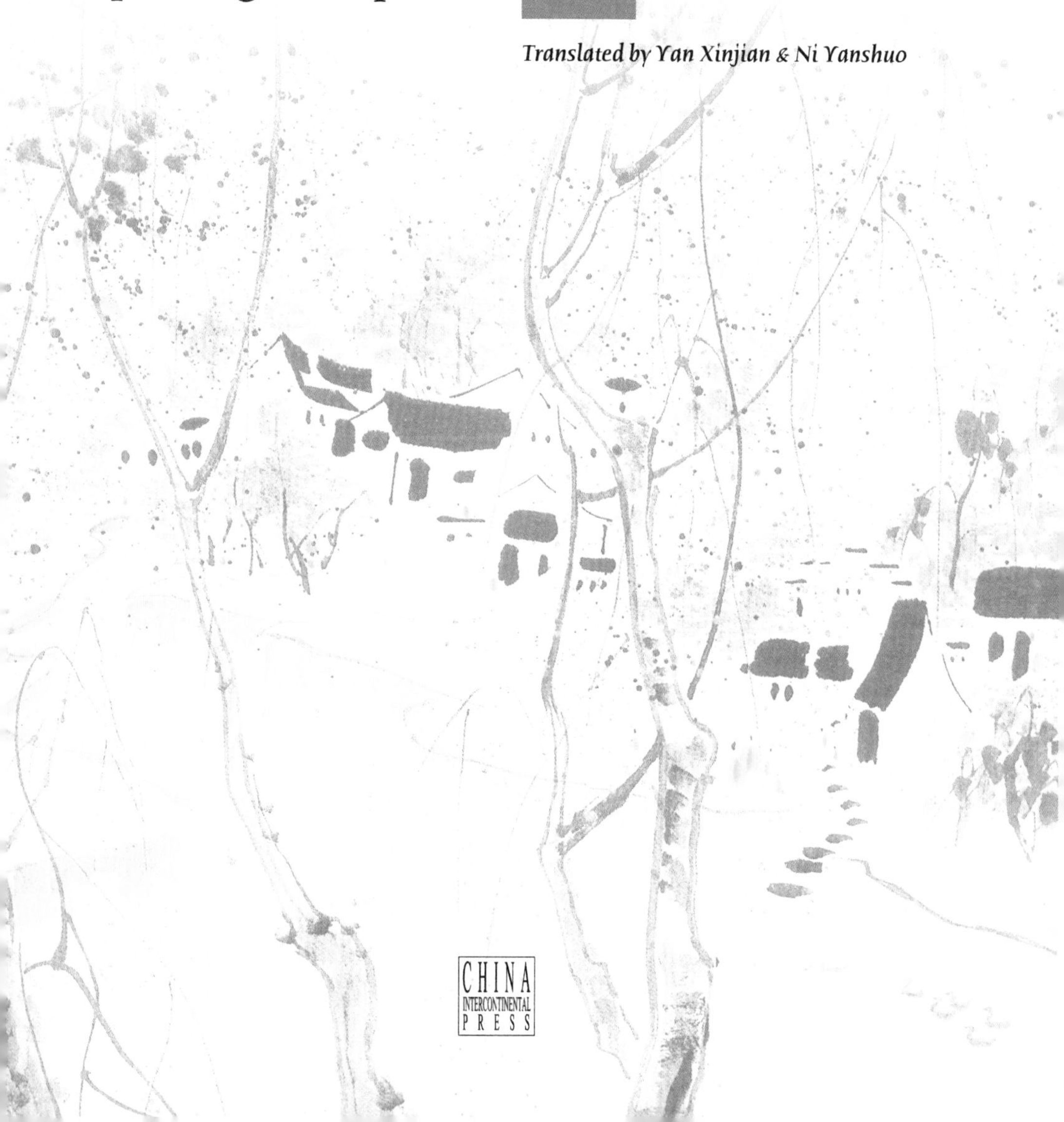

CHINA INTERCONTINENTAL PRESS

图书在版编目（CIP）数据

中国绘画艺术／林茨著；阎新建，倪严硕译．-2版．北京：五洲传播出版社，2010.1
ISBN 978-7-5085-1669-1

Ⅰ．中… Ⅱ．①林… ②阎… ③倪… Ⅲ．绘画史 中国 英文
Ⅳ．J209.2
中国版本图书馆CIP数据核字（2009）第180897号

CHINESE PAINTING
Capturing the Spirit of Nature with Brushes

Author: Lin Ci
Translator: Yan Xinjian & Ni Yanshuo
Executive Editor: Zhang Hong
Art Director: Tang Ni
Publisher: China Intercontinental Press (6 Beixiaomachang, Lianhuachi Donglu, Haidian District, Beijing 100038, China)
Tel: 86-10-58891281
Website: www.cicc.org.cn
Printer: C&C Joint Printing Co., (Beijing) Ltd.
Edition: Jan. 2010, 2nd edition, 3rd print run
Format: 155×230mm 1/16
Price: RMB 99.00 (*yuan*)

Contents

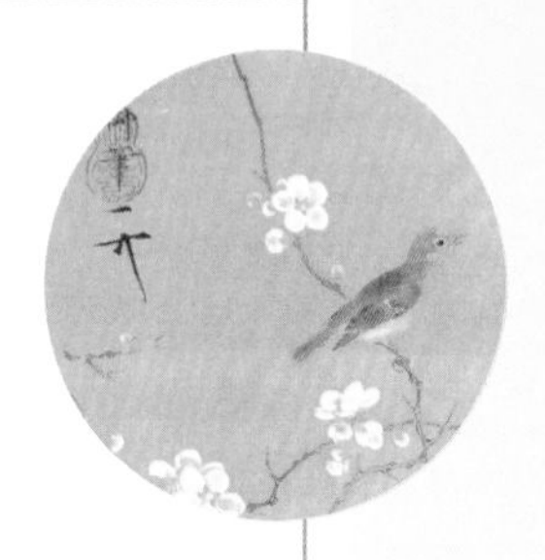

Preface

Yellow River is the cradle of Chinese Civilizations. On the fertile lands along this mother River, tribes settled, clans formed, civilization developed and art emerged. Chinese painting can be dated back to prehistoric times and the earliest paintings of art were found on pottery pieces unearthed from several early civilizations in the Yellow River Valley. For example, Yangshao Civilization around 5000–3000 BC was a great and influencial society with its geographic area reaching today's Hubei Province to the south and Mongolia to the north and was a civilization in a transition period from matriarchal to patriarchal society. Cultivation and agriculture were already extensively used by this civilization. Fine pottery pieces unearthed demonstrated a unique characteristic of their own. The colorful pottery of Majiayao Civilization of early Neolithic time in the upper region of the River around 3000–2000 BC was considered to be the finest in that period and had achieved unprecedented level of sophistication. Another important civilization was Dawenkou Civilization, which was in the lower region of the River around 2300–500

A colored pottery pot of Majiayao Civilization, unearthed from Lintao in Gansu Province.

Fuding You(Wine Cup), late Shang period, (13th to 11th century B.C.), height 35.5cm, inside belly width 26.6 cm, collected by Shanghai Museum.

BC and a typical society in late period of Neolithic time. Collectively they are called color pottery civilizations and many pottery pieces unearthed from the sites associated them have remarkable and colorful paintings and patterns. Composition of the paintings includes human figures, fishes and insects, birds and animals, flowers and plants, and abstract patterns. The advancement of ceramic pottery laid the foundation for the development of bronze civilization and perhaps foretold the arrival of porcelain pottery. Ceramic, bronze and porcelain were all the important carriers of the new art form, paintings. However paintings were only used to decorate their carriers. Artists were anonymous and many of them were tribe women who just settled. Even in bronze and porcelain periods, artists were still craft painters and they were very low in their social rankings. It was very difficult to make a name in history books even for those with finest skills and who served in the imperial court.

Fuding *You* (part).

During the Sui (581–618 AD) and the Tang (618 –907 AD) Dynasties, a system of official examination was developed to select mandarins to serve the empires. Therefore a culture elite class was formed from the early stages of Chinese imperial history. Their ultimate aim was to do the examination well, to be selected and therefore to become a mandarin in order to achieve their political ambitions. In order to reach this ultimate goal they had to read and write thoroughly and extensively in order to become a cultured person and "gentleman" and also to be successful for the examination. Painting and poetry training was a very important part in this endeavour. The greatest Chinese philosopher and scholar, Confucius, said to his fellow students: "ambition must

come from truth (the way); based on integrity; exercised through kindness; expressed through arts." This illustrated that integrity, kindness, and art were an integral part of a true greatness. He also said: "scholar can not be without truth." and "artistic skill is the nearest equivalent to the truth." This demonstrated a logical and underlining similarity between seeking the truth in a spiritual world and practicing a skill in an artistic field. The practice of art had been elevated to resemble the spiritual process of seeking the truth. For them art training was not a simple task just to command a skill but it was a mean to approach the way or the truth.

Consequently there were two types of paintings, those done by craft painters for the sake of painting and those done by scholars as a way of their training to seek the truth. Scholars were the ruling class who controlled the representation to speak for the society. They painted and published books to promote their understanding of painting theory and to discuss their techniques how paintings should be done. Therefore they effectively created criteria by which paintings were judged. And perhaps more importantly, they were more interested in the meaning or theory of painting as they were only using painting as an analogy to seeking the truth. For them, paintings were a mean not an end. It was the process not the end product. Their criteria to judge for a great painter were not only his technique to use pen and brush but also his ability to illustrate he was a great philosopher. From the Song Dynasty (960–1279), it gradually became a popular practice that scholars would use calligraphy of poem to decorate a painting to illustrate its philosophic meanings. This was beyond the ability of an ordinary craft painter, who was normally an uneducated person. The modern artist Huang Binhong (1865–1955) said: calligraphing and drawing follow the same principle, key is at the tip of a writing brush. The various manifestation methods of Han character calligraphy art of Chinese are applied in the drawing works, which is fundamental to the techniques of Chinese drawing.

The career or craft painters even though could have the very finest painting technique, their ability and freedom to express their understanding of painting was limited and their way of painting was very much controlled by others. They normally painted scenes of real life and religion teaching by orders of their employers. They painted figures, landscapes (mountains and rivers, *shanshui*), flowers, fish or insects primarily for decorative purposes. In contrast, the painters who had higher social status would consider painting as an academic activity. It was a mean for them to enjoy the nature. For them, painting was not to imitate the nature but a way to express their philosophic feelings. Mind came before nature. Therefore landscape on their paintings would not be a mechanic copy of beautiful sceneries and it was rather the spiritual combination of their mind and the nature.

Food Vessel with Snail Shape and Beast Skin Pattern, early Western Zhou Dynasty (11th Century BC), height 14.7cm, diameter 18.4cm, collected by Shanghai Museum.

Most paintings of this type were done by those who were well educated. In fact, almost all the culture elites had followed, treasured, and practiced this tradition. Confucius said in his *Analects*: "mountain fulfils the wise and water gratifies the learnt." This may not be a direct comment on paintings but it had directly linked the nature beauty to wisdom and knowledge. This had a very profound effect on painting aesthetics of the generations followed. And his followers even further developed this aesthetic philosophy: "who appreciate the natural beauty are the wise and the learnt." This provided a new philosophical meaning to a seclusion living admired by the culture elite.

Another important system of thought in China is Taoist and *Dao De Jing* (*the Book of the Way*) is a philosophic work by its founder Laozi. The work is also considered an important concise book on painting. Laozi said in his Dao De Jing: "strong voice

appears gentle," "grand shape looks vague," "great skill seams easy."

During the warring state period (475–221 BC) the King of Song Kingdom invited a group of painters to his palace. Almost all the invited painters were overwhelmed by this unexpected event, stood idle, shaking in the court. Only one of them was very relaxed and come later than required, painted without all the unnecessary hesitation and went home after a routine show of courtesy. The King was very impressed and sent a servant to visit him immediately and saw him sitting naked at home without any worry and expectation. The King said he was a true painter.

Another sage applauded as the spiritual leader of the group of Chinese artists is Zhuangzi (about 369–286 BC). Zhuangzi wrote in his *Knowledge Wandering North: Zhuangzi*: "the nature possesses the best beauty" and promoted the ideal to "go with the nature", "inner tranquillity", and "concentrate without distraction". He told the following story in his *A Essay about Tianzi: Zhuangzi* to illustrate his point of view. Zhuangzi considered that a true painter should not be bound by fine details. He should be acting according to his mind and to paint freely. Taoists promoted the philosophy that the simple was the best. Laozi said: "what you see is not what you learn. That is the way of the world." Zhuangzi had a very similar view. He said in *Heaven and Earth: Zhuangzi:* "five colors only make eyes dazzled." According to him (*Constrained in Will: Zhuangzi*), "simplicity is essence without disguise". He strongly believed in "nothing could compete with the beauty of simplicity (*the Way of Heaven: Zhuangzi*)." Both Laozi and Zhuangzi promoted the philosophy of simplicity without unnecessary "five colors". "Sitting naked" was an illustration of inner tranquility and free spirit. It inspired the ink-and-wash freehand to become the ultimate style of Chinese paintings.

The discovery of photography in 1839 caused a panic among the painters in Europe. The primary way of painting in the West was to imitate the nature rather than express it. When they saw an apparatus could do the job better than they could, they felt a sense of despair. Paul Klee (1879–1940) said art started to express the spirit rather the material world from the moment photography was invented. Therefore from 19th century, the western painting started to embark on a new trend of modernism. Ten years after its discovery, photography arrived in China but it never had a same impact on the Chinese painters than it did in the west although the culture elite and the ruling class in China admired the magic power of western painters for their ability to copy nature objects. The royal family of the time, including the grand mother of the Emperor, Cixi, had a tremendous curiosity on the newly arrived technology but they never viewed it as alternative to the art of painting. Traditional Chinese painting was fundamentally an abstract art form. Although there were no absolute abstract Chinese paintings in its original meaning, objects in a painting were not a direct copy of the nature world following the principle of perspective. It was rather a combination or harmony between the nature world and human emotion, a product of "heaven (nature) and human". The effect Chinese painters would like to illustrate in their paintings was not a visual effect of colors and patterns as their Western counterparts would like to achieve. The description of objects in their paintings was no means accurate and few concerned about such factors as colors, principle of perspective, anatomy, surface feel, and relative size. What they would like to achieve was a world in their mind of non materials. The nature world was not an object for them to make a true copy and it was rather elements for them to build their own world.

In contrast to the popular view of western painters, Chinese artists hardly considered the nature as an object but rather a subject which they worshiped. They had an uncontrollable impulse and energy to exemplify through the creation of certain image to prove the multiplicity of the nature in their mind. Remote mountains and running streams were the traces of their thinking process. The 17th century Germany philosopher Leibniz used the words *Naturliche*

Imitating Ni Yunlin's Autumn Water and Lucid Sky (182cm×79.5cm), by Zhang Daqian

Theologie (nature theology) to describe this unique Chinese attitude towards the nature. In his *Dao De Jing*, Laozi considered the nature was the ultimate force.

"Human governed by earth; earth governed by heaven; heaven governed by Dao (the way), Dao ultimately governed by the nature".

This logic of Taoist from human through *Dao* (the way) to the nature clearly demonstrated when artists were painting landscape they were touching the *Dao* through which they ultimately immersed into the nature. This was how the Chinese painters viewed the nature. The nature was not only great and respectful but also lovable and inspirational. It should be respected and eulogized. Also it could be understood and acted upon to serve our purposes. The rules of nature could be used to change how the nature was functioning. In the real world, very often the nature was behind the chores of daily life and could not be seen clearly. When the painters were observing the world they needed to see through and to access its true form in order for their mind to resonate with the nature. The talent of a good painter was also a force of nature, through which the true nature would appear without the disguise and people could feel the vigor of life and the warmth of spiritual world in their paintings.

The intellectual had the political and, for many, administration responsibility but they could not forget the lure of the nature. A landscape would provide a way for them to enjoy natural beauty which they duly missed. Guo Xi (1020–1109 AD), a painter in the Song Dynasty, indicated in his *Spirituality by Forest Stream* (*Linquan Gaozhi*), that intellectuals admired the forests and streams simply because they were the places which they would belong and could not reach. He stipulated that a landscape should be "marchable," "visible," "accessible" and "livable." If a landscape met these criteria it would be a master piece. He wrote: "all the painters should bear this in their mind when they paint and all the art critics should remember this when they judge." This would explain the difference between Chinese landscape paintings and western

Many art critics consider Huang Binhong had a very similar influence in the history of Chinese paintings to that of impressionists in the history of western paintings. He completed the transition of the traditional shanshui to the modern. *Ink and Colored Shanshui*, by Huang Binhong, (102cm x 39cm).

landscape paintings. It was very rare for an ancient Chinese painter to concentrate on the details or a small part of landscape. All Chinese landscapes since the Tang and Song Dynasties not only had mountains and streams but also roads leading to top of mountains, streams by roads intersecting with each other, buildings on mountain ridges, people on road and boats on water. Chinese like to say they "read" a painting. That was to say they appreciated the content of a painting and enjoyed its spiritual meanings.

Guo Xi, also discussed in details the composition for a painting. He wrote, "thousand mile mountains couldn't tell the wonder to the completeness, ten thousand mile rivers still leave out the beauty. A simple outline on the paper is no different from a map." In his view, the composition of landscapes should display the overall view in essence, the "great shape" and "grand view." This was a further development of Taoist theory that "grand shape looks vague." He also compared a painting with a human body: "to mountain water is the artery; grass and plants are hairs; smoking and clouds are colors of life. A mountain becomes live when it has water; it become vivid when it has grasses and plants; and it become vibrant when it has smoking and clouds. To water, mountain is the face; buildings on ridges are the eyes; fishmen by river are the soul. Water becomes charming when it has mountain to decorate; it becomes lucid when it has buildings; it becomes spacious when there are fishmen. This is the essence of composition for landscape."

When humanity and moral values were applied to a painting, it would obviously affect the way a painter viewed the world. Guo Xi used three types of remoteness to illustrate:

"There are three types of remoteness for a mountain. Viewing from bottom to top, it is remoteness in height; viewing from front to back, it is remoteness in depth; viewing from nearby to faraway, it is remoteness in horizon."

"Remoteness in height, in depth, and in horizon" directed our view from a point of painting to where totally beyond and to the "grand view" and to an infinite universe. This carried a symbolic

"Soundless Poems"
Chinese painting is done on rice paper or silk with a brush dipped in black or colored ink. The finished work is then mounted on scrolls, which can be hung or rolled up. Chinese painting features multi-focus perspective, depends on lines and ink color to represent forms and texture, and is often complemented by poems, verses, calligraphy, or carving. Major subject matters featured in Chinese painting include human figures, landscapes, flowers and birds, and animals. There are mainly two techniques in Chinese painting: meticulous and freehand. Since the rise of intellectual painting in the Song and Yuan Dynasties, Chinese painting has become increasingly integrated with poetry, calligraphy and seal carving, and contained inscriptions of varying lengths. Chinese paintings often reflect the painter's emotions and feelings and are representational and philosophical, and are therefore dubbed "Soundless Poems".

meaning of "into the world" and "out of the world." The culture elite would endeavor for most of their life to become mandarins in a material world. This was "into the world". But at the same time they would not like their spirit being spoilt by the temptations of the material world and hoped landscape would give them a sense being pure and lofty. The artistic conception of landscape was closely related with "remoteness." That is "remoteness" symbolized their "out of the world." This philosophy of painting composition satisfied the spiritual gratification of the culture elite. If a painter lost his admiration for the "remoteness" a landscape would become a landscape painting. They should not be bound by details of scenery and compromise their spiritual endeavor.

Chinese artists often say: the whole horse is in the heart, the ripe bamboo is in the heart, the valley is in heart, etc. It means the artists need first command thorough, crisp and deep understanding of the natural existence and vivid memorization of the natural scenery, and then prepare paint and paper to start drawing. With the brush at hand, white paper and bright sky, express the emotion free from the disturbance of the worldly appearance. The silk and paper were viewed as the vague world and an infinite universe at large. The brush and pen were means of their endeavor. They would like the brush and pen to travel freely on silk and paper to reflect their freedom in an infinite universe. Apart from visual content, a landscape must have an implicit meaning. Landscape painters always left much blank space on their composition. These were space for imagination. For example, empty space in water around fish and in the sky around birds, all giving a sense that there was the presence of an ever existing universe.

From Gu Kaizhi to Wu Daozi

Tomb Chamber Paintings

The famous Chinese historian Qian Mu once said, apart from calligraphy the most important form of Chinese arts was paintings. Although the earliest Chinese paintings can be dated back to prehistoric times, most paintings in the Qin (221–206 BC) and Han (206 BC–220 AD) Dynasties were murals and stone carvings in palace and tomb chambers. It was until the Wei (220–265 AD) and Jin Dynasties (265–420 AD) paintings had developed into a more popular art form as silk and paper became more affordable and was gradually used for paintings. This illustrates that the earliest Chinese paintings were used almost exclusively to serve aristocracy and religions. From the Wei and Jin to the Sui and Tang Dynasties, Chinese paintings had a gradually transformation to become more accessible to relatively ordinary people. Since the early paintings of aristocracy and religions were mainly drawn or carved on the walls and floors of religious buildings, tomb chambers and palaces, most paintings of Qing and Han Dynasties disappeared together with the destruction of palaces and temples. A few exceptions are preserved in tomb chambers, which have become the main sources to study paintings of those periods.

Dragon, Phoenix and Beauties, a silk painting unearthed in 1949 from a grave in Chenjia Mountain in Hunan Province, considered to be one of the earliest known Chinese paintings.

Murals in tomb chambers are relatively more difficult to destroy and many of them have survived. But perhaps the most significant paintings which have caught the imaginations of art historians are those painted on silk and buried with dead emperors and aristocrats. *Dragon, Phoenix and Beauties*, a silk painting unearthed in 1949 from a grave in Chenjia Mountain in Hunan Province is one of the earliest known

"Non-Dress", a silk painting unearthed from the Mawangdui Tomb near Changsha.

Chinese paintings. It is estimated to belong to the period of 475–221 BC. After the Xia, Shang and Zhou Dynasties China entered the Spring and Autumn period and the Warring States period when Confucius lived and during which many kingdoms fought for dominance in the land of China. The site where Dragon, Phoenix and Beauties was unearthed was in the middle of the kingdom Chu. As it was painted on silk, it was called "silk painting" (*bo hua*).

Like clay figures buried in graves, paintings were used to accompany and to protect the dead by the practice of witchcraft. Painting as art was not practiced by conscience and deliberation yet. On *Dragon, Phoenix and Beauties* there is a lady in the middle. It is difficult to tell whether it is a witch praying for the deceased or it represents the deceased herself. Above the lady, there are dragon and phoenix, both are fictional figures of ancient China and they are auspicious signs. Like angels in Christian teaching, they are believed to be able to guide the dead to the heaven.

Another important silk painting was unearthed from the Mawangdui Tomb near Chanshan. It is estimated to belong to the period around 165 BC. The painting is in a T-shape. Archaeologists call it "non-dress" painting as it looks like a dress but could not be worn. Composition of the painting depicts "a soul going to heaven." The top section of the painting clearly represents the heaven, the middle section is the earth and the low section is underground scene. Reality is mixed with fantasy. The middle earth section tells the story of the person buried. She was the wife of Licang, an aristocrat. She dresses in very colorful lavish silk cloth. Judging from her composure, she looks like an old person. She is walking through a large hall with servants kneeling in front of her and maids following her behind. Slightly below this, there is a banqueting scene but without the presence of the master. The banqueting tables are packed with luxury dishes and plates with delicious foods and glass full of wines. As there is no master present, all the people are not eating and drinking but are standing and bow forward as if they would see the master off. Symbolically she is sent off to the heaven by all her servants and maids. The top heaven section is full of imagination and romantical fantasy. The traditional belief in the Han period was that a person died his or her soul would go to heaven and become a celestial being in another world. The celestial world in the painting has the Sun, the Moon and stars above. There is a golden horse on the Sun and jade rabbit on the Moon, two auspicious animals which people in the Han period considered to be associated with the Sun and the Moon. Also seen is a large mulberry tree shinning in moonlights and a dragon flying through sky. Under moonlight, a young woman flies with the dragon. She looks as if she has eventually escaped the chores of earthly life and totally rejuvenated, dancing with dragon in a celestial world.

This wonderful Han period silk painting carried the tradition which we see first on the silk painting *Dragon, Phoenix and Beauties* of the Warring State period. All characters on the painting have only showed their side profiles. Chinese ancestors believed that a person's side profile could demonstrate more of his or her characteristics. The Han silk painting is more sophisticated than the silk painting of the Warring State period. The latter only has simple lines of drawings showing symbolic meanings. Though it carries the symbolic tradition, the Han painting has used more elegant lines of drawing and fine composition to depict an imaginative and romantic story on earth and in heaven. It has adopted "non dress" format to show the direction of painting, from the top to the bottom, the heaven, the earth and the under world. In the middle section of the earthly life, we could also see time direction of the present and the past. The present is above the past. The Han painting also shows more elegant and sophisticated drawing technique. It uses black ink to draw an outline and add colors on spaces in between afterwards. The mineral pigments of cinnabar red, malachite green, azurite blue and chalk white on the painting still have remarkable original colors more than two thousands of years later.

The Most Romantic Painting

The Han dynasty began to employ royal painters to serve in the imperial court. They were not allowed to paint outside the palaces. The Emperors also built special pavilions to store the royal collections of paintings which mainly illustrated the contribution and achievement emperors had made during their reigns. All the dynasties ever since had kept this tradition until the last emperor of the Qing Dynasty. One of the important tasks for the royal painters was to draw portraits of many wives and court ladies so the emperor could use those portraits to select which one to accompany him for the night. As consequences, many court ladies would bribe royal painters to paint a portrait looked more beautiful than they actually were. There was a famous fable of the Han dynasty which told the story of royal painter Mao Yanshou. When he was severing at the Han court, he met one of the most beautiful women in Chinese history, Wang Zhaojun. She did not bribe Mao and so the emperor never asked her accompany during her entire stay at the court. Even worse the emperor gave her away to marry the king of Xiongnu when he came to the Han capital to seek peace with the empire. When the emperor finally saw her just before her departure to Xiongnu, he found Wang Zhaojun was the most beautiful woman he ever saw. The emperor was very furious and investigated why he did not call her accompany. He found her portrait. One legend said Mao Yanshou was executed by the emperor.

This incident illustrates that painters in the Han Dynasty were still very low in their social status and painting was only a mean to earn a living. Even royal painters were still a slave in the imperial court and their destiny was in the control of their master, the emperor.

After the fall of the Han Dynasty and the rise of the Wei and Jin Dynasties, many social changes started during this period. Two of the most significant were the arrival of Buddhism and foreign cultures, and the emergence of an active intellectual class. During the Wei Jin Southern and Northern Dynasties China divided small states, and political upheavals across the country. However Buddhism prospered tremendously during this period and reached an unprecedented level of acceptance. Because of the wide spread of Buddhism, many caves of religion importance were carved and temples were built. Their creation required many painters to decorate them with murals. Consequently painting technique was developed very rapidly. At the same time, social upheavals brought the dissolution of the intellectuals. They sought refuges in Buddhism and seclusion metaphysics to escape the social and political reality. This was a period when many famous scholars established their places in the culture history of China. For example, Ji Kang (224–263 AD) was, like many other scholars in that period, good at poetry and painting as well as music and chess. Wang Xizhi (321–379 or 303–361 AD) was the most representative scholar of them all. Today he is considered to be the Calligraphy Saga. Other famous scholar painters of that period included Cao Buxing, Cao Zhongda, Dai Kui, Gu Kaizhi, and Lu Tanwei. Unfortunately few of their work have survived.

One exception is Gu Kaizhi and his paintings. None of Gu Kaizhi's original works has survived, but he has still acquired a legendary status, both as a painter and as a writer on Chinese painting. He was given extensive coverage in the dynastic histories and the seminal text on painting, *Famous Paintings Record of Past Dynasties* (*Li-dai ming-hua ji*) written by Zhang Yanyuan (about 815–875 AD). Since he was one of the most famous painters of that period, his paintings were copied by many in generations after his death to learn his technique. Today his paintings are known mainly through copies of the Tang period.

Gu Kaizhi (346–407 AD) was born in Wuxi Jiangsu Province and first painted in Nanjing, the capital of the Eastern Jin. Legend said he was devoted but shrewd, humorous and boastful but honest and direct. He was a man of contradictions, typical of scholars of the Wei and Jin Dynasties. He was born a noble man and had been appointed as various officials with little responsibility. But for most of his life, he worked as advisers in the households of very important officials. During his early years, he never shied away from his friends of skillful craft painters and stayed away as much as possible from the pursuing of his political ambitions. He devoted much of his early time to painting. When he was only 20 years old he started to paint murals for Buddhist temples and become a well known painter. Many of his paintings are recorded in imperial archives of the Tang and Song Dynasties but there are only four paintings known to us and all of them are copies. Nevertheless they are still very important paintings. Among the four paintings,

Nymph of the Luo River scroll (27.1cm×572.8cm), ink and color on silk (part), attributed to Gu Kaizhi, collected by Beijing Palace Museum.

The Admonitions of the Instructress to the Court Ladies and *Nymph of the Luo River* are the most known.

The Admonitions of the Instructress to the Court Ladies was completed in the Western Jin period (209–306 AD) to illustrate a political parody written by Zhang Hua (about 232–300 AD). The Admonition by Zhang Hua is an article written to promote the Confucianism's values and it takes a moralizing tone, attacking the excessive behaviour of an Empress Jia to teach court ladies the moral virtues of being a lady. With reference to the stories in the article Gu Kaizhi illustrated all characters of emperor, empress and court ladies in the story. The protagonist is the court instructress who guides the ladies of the imperial harem on correct behaviour. There are two copies survived. A copy of the Tang Dynasty arrived at the British Museum in 1903 and the other, a copy of the Song

Dynasty is kept at the Beijing Palace Museum. *The Admonitions Scroll*, a copy of Tang period has nine scenes, but it is now incomplete; the first two scenes are missing, as well as the text to the first scene.Each section has the original story written on the painting. This painting has been executed in a fine linear style that is typical of fourth-century figure painting. Similar pictorial motifs have been discovered in contemporary tombs. Texts describe Gu Kaizhi as having painted in this manner. The inscriptions and seals on this scroll date back to the eighth century, when this copy of Gu's original was probably painted.

Nymph of the Luo River illustrates a romantic poem of the same title written by Cao Zhi, the younger brother of the Wendi emperor of the Wei Dynasty. In the painting, Gu Kaizhi transformed the feeling of poet into a touchable visual displace. Standing by the

Luo River, Cao Zhi stares at Nymph on the other side of the river. He could see but could not touch, all the lingering and despair. Nymph on the other side of river seems to walk slowly over clouds and ripples towards him, so elegant and romantic. Wind blows gently across and the river drifts vigorously along, so vivid and dramatic. The painting has created a perfect visual poetic story, combined reality with imagination, and mixed fairytales with earthly life.

The silk paintings unearthed since the Warring State period and Han Dynasty illustrate the basic traditional Chinese painting technique which use black ink to sketch and add colors afterwards to fill the spaces in between. The paintings of Gu Kaizhi are a further extension of these early techniques and a perfection of Chinese painting format. Zhang Yanyuan, a Tang Dynasty art historian, described the paintings by Gu Kaizhi as "compact without interruption, repetitive with transcendence, stylish with variety, and swift as thunder". Like calligraphy of Wang Xizhi, the lines drawn by the painter not only illustrate figures and subjects but also themselves have a rigorous structure and rich rhythm, showing the beauty of structure and composition. The court ladies, the mountains and the shooting scene on his painting are almost a direct copy of conceptual techniques used on silk paintings from the Han Dynasty. This does not suggest that Gu Kaizhi was not an imaginative and creative painter. It is rather the conceptual formula had become habitual and compulsory already during his time. Like calligraphy has its own rules of writing, the command of conceptual formula in painting is a symbol of accomplishment in art training. However because mountains, stones, trees and other large

18 Mansion Gods scroll (28cm×491cm) (part), attributed to Zhang Cengyao of the Southern Dynasty, collected by Osaka Municipal Museum of Art.

subjects are also drawn in a single line in this traditional technique, the sizes of figures and other natural subjects in a painting would loss their visual perspective in comparison. This would generally indicate that the technique used in Chinese landscape paintings of the Wei and Jin period was still in its infancy as far as overall view was concerned and needed further refinement. As a great artist of that generation, Gu Kaizhi analyzed and refined the good elements of painting of that period and used them creatively. This makes his work an example of exceptional excellence and many painters in the generations followed have copied his paintings to learn these refined techniques. His style and technique of painting can be found on the paintings by artists Zhan Ziqian and Wu Daozi of the Sui and Tang periods.

"Communication of the Soul"

Until the later years of the Han dynasty, intellectuals were not involved with paintings. By the time of the Wei Jin period, it was relatively common for the culture elite to participate in painting and share the art form with the professional craft painters. Because of the participation of the culture elite, the discussion of theory on paintings became possible. Gu Kaizhi was a self conscious practitioner of Chinese painting and in his all the techniques of that period assembled. He was also a pioneering theorist on paintings. He wrote three books on painting theory, *On Painting, Introduction to the Famous Paintings of the Wei and Jin Dynasties* and *Painting Yuntai Mountain*. In these works, he for the first time proposed the theory of "communication of the soul" and promoted that the deciding factor of good painting was whether it "communicating the soul". In *On Painting* he said:

"Soul belongs to the other world and it is the entirety of endeavour."

"The beauty of shape; the dimension of body; the shade of yin and yang, the line of sketch; all are common features of the nature world. The spirit and rhythm however are in the mind. If the hands can represent the

eyes of a painter, the reward of communication is beyond comprehension."

The Wei Jin period was a time when the Buddhism metaphysics was the fashion of the cultured society. However Gu Kaizhi was a painter of simplicity. Although communication of soul or creation of rhythm was the goal of painting, Gu insisted this could only be achieved by coping nature and pursuing shapes and contents. Therefore he considered it was necessary to study "the beauty of shape, the dimensions of body, the shade of *yin* and *yang*, and the line of sketch". The communication of soul and rhythm could only be achieved by mean of shape and subject. He considered achieving the entirety of this harmony once or twice even painting thousands of times was a reward from heaven. He wrote: "In figure paintings the clothes and the belongings are not very important. The spirit, composure, and poise are more essential. The eyes are the spirit and the decisive factor". He also mentioned "bone feature method" and "balance of composition" in *On Painting*. He believed that body bone features was a reflection of the inner spirit of rhythm. Composition balance meant the choice of the subjects and the relationship of subjects in a painting.

The Six Dynasties (220–589 AD) were a period when the fundamental Chinese painting aesthetic standards were developed and it was also an active period of painting critics. The painting philosophy of Gu Kaizhi was summarised by an art critics of that period, Xie He (479–502 AD) into the six painting principles. They were "give life to body"; "ink sketch by bone features"; "apply rhythm to shape"; "paint color by type"; "balance composition by relationship" and "copy by transcendence." "Give life to body" was the primary important rule. First these principles were written applicable to figure painting and were universally adopted. Communication of soul or rhythm had become the ultimate criteria to judge a painting. Thereafter the rules have been also extended to the paintings of landscape, and bird and flower.

Spring Outing (You-Chun TU)

The painting style of the Sui Dynasty had a transitional characteristic from the old to the new and it was refined and beautiful. Many painters during that period assembled in the Capital and most were good at paintings of religious subjects. The other popular topic then was the life of aristocracy. Landscape developed into an independent style of painting during the Sui Dynasty after relative positions and ratios of landscape objects were properly addressed.

Zhan Ziqian (550–604 AD) lived through the North Qi and North Zhou Dynasties and after the Sui reunited China, he served as adviser and administrator to the imperial court. Historians commented that his paintings were fine in details and colorful in completion. He was a natural successor to Gu Kaizhi. In *the Admonitions of the Instructress to the Court Ladies* and *Nymph of the Luo River* Gu employed sketch lines looked like silk threads coming out silkworms. This fine technique was imitated by Zhan Ziqian in his painting *Spring Out* which helped to create a wonderful and magnificent landscape with crisp lucid lines as smooth as silk. Before Zhan Ziqian, landscape had not been developed into an independent style of painting. Like Gu, Zhan was a well developed painter but he would prefer to draw scenes of the nature world. *Xuanhe Collection of Paintings* wrote he had "a special talent of creating distance and space within a few inches of drawings". He was a master to use space to express the beauty and rhythm of landscape. He is considered to be the first person painting in the true style of shanshui. He inherited the tradition of the Wei and Jin period and foretold a new style of the generation to come. Especially his landscape style had profound effect on the paintings during Tang and Song Dynasties. Painting critics of Yuan Dynasty, Tang Hou commented that he was the father of paintings for the Tang Dynasty.

After passing through many hands, the original *Spring Outing*

Spring Outing (43cm×80.5cm) scroll, ink and color on silk, attributed to Zhan Ziqian, collected by Beijing Palace Museum.

has survived. It is the only piece by Zhan Zqian and is the earliest Chinese painting scroll survived. It is also the first true landscape painting known to us. On the front there is the writing "*Spring Outing* by Zhan Ziqian". The painting is subsequently in the collections of well-known connoisseurs who added their own seals and inscriptions, for example, the imperial seal of the Huizong emperor of the Song Dynasty, the inscriptions of the Qianlong emperor of the Qing Dynasty and the seals of imperial court and other collectors. The painting is drawn mainly using green and dark blue and it is about a spring outing by a group of aristocrats. The sketch lines are fine and smooth but full of strength. The colors are bright and lucid. People and horses are tiny but full of details. The paintings have changed the way how a painting is composed. The original use of landscape in a painting was only to emphasise characters. It marks the beginning of independent style of Shanshui.

The paining is about spring outing by a group of aristocrats. There are exuberant fields with luxuriant spring sunshine.

Mountains stand on the background. Ripples of water show the reflection of light. Lucid plants have announced the arrival of spring. Clouds fly smoothly anmd lazily through the mountains. Embankment extends into the distance. An arch bridge can be vaguely seen at background. Gentlemen are riding horses and walking and ladies are boating in the lake, all towards the waterfall in the centre of the painting. It is drawn from a bird's eye view from the top. The near and far sections come focused towards the middle section, which has helped to create a rhythm of harmony with full depth of the painting. Composition is constructed along a diagonal line across from the bottom left to the top right, and it is also the direction of spring water running through the painting with mountains and embankment on each side of this invisible line, full of live and vibrancy of spring. The use of green and blue illustrates the spring colors of plants and trees. This has formed its own unique characteristic and is called "blue and green style." The other dominant color is golden yellow. Therefore this style is further developed and called "golden green landscape" (*jin bi shanshui*). All the mountains, plants and stones have sketch lines only and spaces are filled with colors. The lines are very fine but full of variety.

Most art historians agreed that *Spring Outing* had marked a new era of Chinese painting and ended the traditional view that "characters should be larger than mountain and water can not cover major part of a painting." During the Han Dynasty and the period of Gu Kaizhi, landscape appeared in a painting mostly in an abstract form. In the landscape painting of Zhan Ziqian, people can see his efforts to try to restore the order of nature. While admiring the wonderful nature in exuberant and lucid spring, the painter suddenly realized the original place human should occupy and his relationship to the nature world should be. He used many mineral pigments for the painting. However in comparison to the silk painting of the Han period, he almost used realistic spot coloring to contrast the distance between different subjects rather than the

traditional abstract technique of level brushing which he only used to paint clouds around the mountains. The balance of the two created a realistic vivid world with a dreamily sensation.

As the earliest painting of nature, *Spring Outing* has all the basic elements of Chinese landscape painting. It is marchable, visible, accessible and livable. It is a textbook painting, meeting all the rules of landscape as set by Guo Xi in his *Spirituality by Forest Stream*: "to mountain water is the artery; grasses and plants are hairs; smoking and clouds are colors of life. A mountain becomes live when it has water; it becomes vivid when it has grasses and plants; and it becomes vibrant when it has smoking and clouds. To water, mountain is the face; buildings on ridges are the eyes; fishmen by river are the soul. Water becomes charming when it has mountain to decorate; it becomes lucid when it has buildings; it becomes spacious when there are fishmen. This is the essence of composition for shanshui." As an early painter of realism for simplicity, Zhan Ziqian had clearly demonstrated the realism intention in his *Spring Outing*. This is a clear contrast to the view of artists in the Yuan period to blindly emphasize the subjective way of painting the nature. He perhaps had been influenced by an actual event or a particular experience he had, which made him have a desire to reflect his personal experience through a painting. For example he used ripples to reflect the gentle breezes and spot coloring of green stones and lucid flowers to announce the arrival of spring. His color landscape has both elements of so called "blue and green *shanshui*" and "ink and wash *shanshui*". But both elements are not very obvious. To some extent, this indicates a confusion of his generation before a perfect harmony of realism intention and expression method is found.

Emperors of Great Prosperity

The Tang Dynasty inherited and continued many painting traditions of the Sui Dynasty. It had a period of comprehensive

< *Eight Gentlemen Spring Out* (161cm×103cm), attributed to Zhao Yan of the Five Dynasties period, collected by Taipei Palace Museum.

Playing Chess behind a Screen scroll (40.3cm×70.5cm), ink and color on silk, attributed to Zhou Wenju, collected by Beijing Palace Museum.

advancements in many key areas of paintings, such as the accomplishment of saddle horse characters, the maturity of blue and green landscape and ink and wash landscape by inheriting and improving the compact style of the Sui period, the creation of a new painting genre of flowers and birds. The most important of all was the rise of portrait painting. Several painters started to establish themselves as leading specialists of the newly created painting genre, flower and bird paintings. Another significant trend was the localization of religious paintings to depict many elements of ordinary life.

Although *Spring Outing* by Zhan Ziqian created a new painting style and provided enjoyments for many generations to come, landscape was not in the main stream of paintings during the period of great prosperity of the Tang Dynasty (618–917 AD). The Emperors still viewed paintings as a way to enhance their control on the country and to maintain their superiority on arts. To serve this purpose portrait and figure paintings of royal, religious and historical significance had arisen to an unprecedented importance. Yan Liben, a noble man by birth, was one of the most prominent painters of portraits and figures. He was not only a famous painter who created many characters from history books but also a royal architecturer and engineer. Once he was the chief engineer for the imperial court, in charge of building and manufacture. Although he was a painter of such prominence, he still felt inadequate and inferior in the society. He told his descendents that when he was young he also read extensively and no less than those who went to become a mandrian. But instead he chose to excel in the field of painting and was still treated like a servant even after he became such a prominent painter so he advised them not to follow.

Under the instruction of the Taizong emperor of the Tang Dynasty, he completed the paintings of *Thirteen Emperors from Han to Sui, Eighteen Scholars of Qin Household, Twenty-four Heroes in Linyan Pavilion, Imperial Palanquin,* and *Court Officials* (*zhi gong tu*), among which, *Thirteen Emperors from Han to Sui* and *The Imperial Palanquin* have survived.

The Thirteen Emperors are the portraits of thirteen emperors from the Han to Sui Dynasties, including the Guangwudi Liu Xiu of the Han Dynasty (in the reign from 25–57 AD), the Wendi Cao Pei of the Wei Dynasty (in the reign from 220–226 AD), King Sun Quan of the Kingdom of Wu (in the reign from 222–252 AD), the Wudi Sima Yan of the Jin Dynasty (in the reign from 265 to 290 AD), who were the founders of a dynasty, and the last king of the Kingdom Chen (in the reign from 583–587 AD), and the Yandi of the Sui Dynasty (in the reign from 605–616 AD), who lost an empire. All the empire founders look solemn, benevolent and incomparable graceful while all the empire losers look dejected and apathetic. The rulers of the Tang Dynasty would like to teach their descendants that how an empire was built and lost. These portraits are very political. In this Yan Liben excelled as a royal painter appointed by the Taizong emperor (in the reign from 627–649 AD). Although each individual

The Imperial Palanquin scroll (38.5cm×129cm), ink and color on silk, attributed to Yan Liben, collected by Beijing Palace Museum.

of these portraits are unique, the formula adopted since the Han Dynasty are followed, for example the posture of emperors can be traced back to that in Nymph of the Luo River and murals of the Tang Dynasty in Dunhuang.

The other important work of Yan Liben is *the Imperial Palanquin,* which records the grand occasion of envoys from Tubo (in the present-day Tibet) coming to Chan'an (present-day Xi'an),the Tang Capital, to ask for the permission to marry Princess Wencheng in 490 AD. Since this was an actual royal event which provided abundant contents for the painting, the final result is vivid and realistic which has avoided the abstract conceptual elements of and showed a true artistic creativity. On the bottom right, there is the imperial sedan carried by court ladies on which sit the Taizong emperor. On his left there are three ceremony masters and in the middle, the emissary named Lu Dong Zan and on the back a court attendant. The Taizong emperor is the focus of the painting. He sits on the royal sedan, looks solemn with a perfect composure and graceful with a deep forward sight, full of majesty of an emperor in the reign of great prosperity. There are nine court ladies altogether, carrying the sedan, and holding large overhead fans and a red round parasol of silk, each with unique posture, adding lucid color and beauty to a very politic scene. Their enchanting tenderness and breezing gaits and posture are in a great contrast to the radiant majesty and solemn determination of the Taizong emperor. The Tubo envoys are shown as smaller in stature, looking submissive and eager. The painting has no background view and is composed entirely with characters. The geometry and composition are compact and from the right to the left, with clear focus, distinct rhythm, crisp and strong colors with large areas of red and green in alternation, and full of rhythm and bright visual impact. It is a perfect combination of highly decorative dimensional geometry and realism representation of individual characters. All the characters are unique and distinctive. It shows a great deal of the painter's ability and skill on portrait painting, the graceful and majestic Taizong emperor, the foreign looking Tubo envoys, and the submissive court masters and interpreter with their gestures in accordance with their status. The random standing court ladies are gracefully balanced by the symmetric column of court masters, giving a sense of a great official event and also providing a counter balance and contrast to the main character of the painting, the Taizong emperor in the centre.

The Imperial Palanquin is included in *Xuanhe Collection of Paintings* which was compiled under the supervision of the Huizong emperor of the Song Dynasty, Painting History by famous painter Mi Fu (1050–1107 AD) and other numerous art works. It has remained a favorite item for imperial collection and art collectors alike and is considered to represent the highest level of excellence achieved in the early Tang period. *The Imperial Palanquin* currently in Beijing Palace Museum is a copy from the Song Dynasty. Yan Liben continued the exquisite painting style of Gu Kaizhi and Zhan Ziqian. However, he deviated somehow from over emphasis on the deliberate use of elegant liberal lines to depict a sense of moving

Thirteen Emperors from Han to Sui scroll, attributed to Yan Liben, ink and color on silk, collected by Boston Museum of Fine Arts.

with gentle wind. Instead he used more solid and simplistic lines but more representative and responsive to subjects concerned, which art critics call "the iron lines". For the palette of colors, he extensively used cinnabar red and malachite green to emphasize symmetric composition of a painting and to illustrate the elegance of royal status. Only has the Song copy survived today but through which his originality of elegance is still vividly evident.

Another Figure Painting

Aesthetic standards of beauty in the Tang Dynasty are uniquely different to that of today, a constant dinner table talking point especially when modern living has brought so much pressure to maintain the standards of today. They appreciated the beauty of rich and luxurious living and admired full and plump bodies of court ladies. The many sculptures and paintings survived from that period provide a glimpse into this aesthetic standard. The so called "*Qiluo* Characters" often portrayed in the arts have the representative characteristics of this aesthetic standard, with a full and plump body, chubby cheek, curved eyebrows, thin eyes, relaxed postures, and fulfilled and happy facial expressions. The historians consider they were a reflection of opulent livings led by the imperial and noble houses and it was also the fashion imitated by the general public at large.

The most famous painters associated with *Qiluo* Characters are Zhang Xuan (date of birth unknown and active career period was from 713–755 AD) and Zhou Fang (date of birth also unknown and two active career periods were from 766–799 and from 785–804 AD). During the reign of the Xuanzong emperor (712–755 AD), Zhang Xuan had served as a royal painter and he was famous for his skill on figure paintings. Records indicate he was also keen to explore various ways to paint other subjects such as pavilions, forests, birds and flowers. But he was most devoted to depict court ladies of opulent and rich livings. His paintings are associated with many social activities such as spring out, snow day sightseeing, dressing up, hiding and seeking, and music instrument playing. Zhou Fang was born into an aristocrat family. *Xuanhe Collection of Paintings* wrote: "he often visited the rich and beautiful and was good at painting nobles with opulent living, depicting the beauty of plumpness." Both of their works have been among the favourites for collection by the emperors of many dynasties, especially the artist Huizong emperor of the Song Dynasty. He collected seventy or so works of Zhou Fang alone. Only through his copies, do we still have the opportunity to see the most representative paintings of Zhang Xuan, *Guo State Queen Spring Out* and *Court Ladies Preparing for the Newly Woven Silk*.

Guo State Queen Spring Out is a magnificent scroll. The painting was completed during a time when it was fashionable to pursuing

Court Ladies Preparing Newly Woven Silk scroll (37cm×145.3cm), attributed to Emperor Huizong, a copy of Zhang Xuan's painting of the same title, collected by Boston Museum of Fine Arts.

new trends and styles to depict the newly found confidence and prosperity of the Tang Dynasty. However Zhang Xuan adopted a more realism approach for the painting, resonating with the epic poem of Du Fu "the Beauty". It describes an occasion when Guo State Queen went on a sightseeing tour. A column of saddle horses and their riders stroll along and are randomly packed to various small groups. The painting is focused to depict the figures portrayed, using strong but slim lines and balanced colors, rich bright but fresh and elegant, meticulous but without dullness. Gua State Queen are elegantly dressed and accompanied by servants and court ladies, enjoying the sights of a spring day out. There are nine characters in the painting, eight horses, and a baby carried by a court lady, adding some vivid breezes of life into the picture. The Tang Dynasty is renowned for the love of saddle horses, from the emperors, court ladies, and noblemen to court officials alike. Zhang Xuan displayed a great deal of skill in painting horses and earned himself a famous reputation for the talent. The red horse ridden by Quo State Queen is so vividly portrayed and is given a special name Hualiu by historians, like his master, radiating grace and elegance.

In comparison to *Guo State Queen Spring Out, Court Ladies*

Preparing for the Newly Woven Silk depicts a more ordinary life but all court ladies in the painting are still full of the rich and plump postures, another representative painting of *Qiluo Characters*. The court ladies are preparing for the newly woven silk and grouped according to the tasks they are performing, spinning, weaving, and ironing. There are twelve court ladies in the picture, elder and young, sitting and standing, all with distinctive looks. Some are sleeves up and holding pestles, weaving lady is totally focused on silk, some are pushing up and backwards to straightening silk fabrics, a young girl is fanning up a burning fire, and another is watching ironing silk. All of them are luridly and vividly portrayed, showing such an exquisite attitude of the painter. On the front of scroll there is the hand writing by the Zhangzong emperor of the Jin kingdom, *A Copy of Zhang Xuan's Court Ladies Prepaing for Newly Woven Silk* together with marks of his "Mingchang Seven seal". The court ladies portrayed in the painting are all properly dressed up with elegance and grace in a clear contrast to the pleasantry depiction in most paintings of similar topics during the Han and Tang Dynasties. He had added spiritual elegant into ordinary secular life.

Zhou Fang was a painter of many talents. According to *Famous*

Court Ladies with Fans scroll (33.7cm×204.8cm), ink and color on silk, part, attributed to Zhou Fang, collected by Beijing Palace Museum.

Paintings Record of Past Dynasties and *Xuanhe Collection of Paintings*, he was particularly good at painting *Qiluo* Characters and a specialist on portraits. He was also an accomplished religious painter. His the *Relaxed Mother Buddhisattva of Water and Moon* is a fine example of his accomplishments in this regard. The Huizong emperor of the Song Dynasty was a keen collector of his works, particularly his paintings on court ladies. Today we only know many of his paintings through the copies of the Huizong emperor. The aesthetic conception of the *Court Ladies with Fans* is very similar to *Preparing for the Newly Woven Silk*. But the busy working scene of *Preparing for the Newly Woven Silk* has been replaced with a contrasting leisurely story of bored courting ladies. There are sixteen of them in the painting, through their individual postures and related activities, depicting vividly their sense of loneliness and melancholy in the imperial court. The court ladies portrayed by Zhou Fang are more luxurious, dispirited and plump than most

A Copy *of* Zhang Xuan's *Guo State Queen Spring Out* scroll (52cm×148cm), ink and color on paper, attributed to Emperor Huizong, collected by Liaoning Museum.

paintings of his time. Some, then and after his death, have criticised he went to too extreme to depict the *Qiluo* Characters to the extent of distortion and had ignored a basic aesthetic standard. However the aesthetic standard is influenced by the social values and perceptions of the period and his paintings are a reflection of the fashion and luxurious livings of a dynasty at its peak of prosperity. We can only admire his artistic talent. With the fall of its prosperity and the Empire itself eventually, this aesthetic standard and the fashion associated had gone for ever.

The meticulous, rich, and luxurious characteristics of court ladies paintings were gradually extended to the other types of paintings, for example, shanshui, flowers and birds, and religious paintings during the Tang Dynasty. Chines paintings are normally classified into categories by subjects it depicts and each painter would devote to one particular branch to excel. For example, *Famous Paintings Record of Past Dynasties* alone has collected paintings of more than 70 flower and bird specialists. Because of their love for horses, "Saddle Horse Characters" were another important subject for paintings during the Tang Dynasty. Cao Ba, a Tang painter, (date of birth unknown, his active career period

Han Xizai Throwing an Evening Party Scroll (28.7cm×335.5cm), by Gu Hongzhong of the Five Dynasties period, ink and color on silk, collected by Beijing Palace Museum.

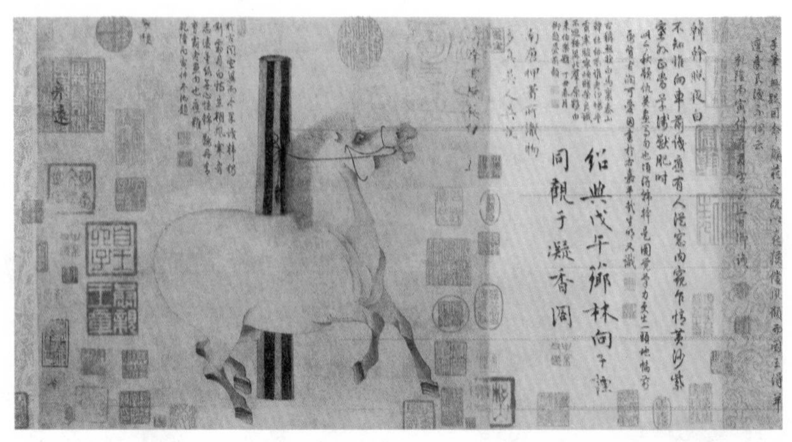

Night-Shining White scroll (30.8cm×33.5cm), by Han Gan, ink on paper, collected by Metropolitan Museum of Art, New York.

Five Buffalos scroll (20.8cm×139.8cm), by Han Huang, collected by Beijing Palace Museum.

was from 713–741 AD), is most renowned for his painting on horses. The great poet, Du Fu, once wrote in his poem to General Cao Ba, the famous *Jade Flower Piebald Horse* in his painting was like a dragon dancing in the celestial heaven and his skill drove all the horses on other paintings to vanish. Han Gan (date of birth unknown) were the student of Cao Ba, born in Chan'an and lived during the reign of the Xuanzong emperor. He worked in a winery during his youth and met the famous poet and painter Wang Wei (701–761 AD) who helped him financially learn to paint. He excelled after ten years of hard training and was good at portraits, figures, ghosts and celestial beings, and particularly horses. As a leading horse painter of the Tang Dynasty, he was known for portraying not only the physical likeness of a horse but also its spirit. Du Fu in another poem of his said: "Han Gan painting horses with love on tips of his brush." The original copy of his painting *Night-Shining White* is in the collection by the

Metropolitan Museum of Arts in the United States of America. Jade Flower Piebald and Night-Shining White were both the names of the favourite chargers of the emperor Xuanzong. The fiery-tempered steed, with its burning eye, flaring nostrils, and dancing hooves, epitomizes Chinese myths about imported "celestial steeds" that "sweat blood" and were really dragons in disguise. This sensitive, precise drawing, reinforced by delicate ink shading, is an example of "baihua" (white painting) a term used in Tang texts on painting to describe monochrome painting with ink shading, as opposed to full color painting. The horses in Han Gan's paintings appear strong and sturdy, and divinely beautiful, with meticulous composition. His horses also seem to inherit the fashion of the period, looking plump and corpulent but muscular. To some extent, they resemble a lovely imagine of family pet. His other important painting is the *Shepherd Horses*, depicting a knight riding a white horse, strolling along and on his right another black horse, a typical painting of "Saddle Horse Characters" with strong but fine meticulous sketch lines, and contrast but complimentary colors. The painting once was collected by the imperial households during the South Tang Dynasty and the Xuanhe period during the reign of the Huizong emperor, with a Huizong's hand writing on the painting, "the original copy by Zhou Fang."

Han Huang (723–787 AD) painted Five Buffalos and the masterpiece was considered as a "rare treasure of all periods" by artists and critics during the Yuan Dynasty. Han Huang was an amateur painter while his main occupations were agriculturist and court official. His speciality was countryside scenes, and farmers and farming animals. His Five Buffalos is painted on a long paper scroll and they are separately drawn, each with a unique vivid posture, grazing quietly along, running with head up, mooring with leg stretched, licking at back, and gently strolling along, and no figures on the painting. All of them look joyful and contented. The composition is balanced and proper ratio and perspective are followed. The sketch lines are simple and solid, and full of varieties. Color is light but depicting a strong sense of heaviness. The whole picture is splendid and lavishly beautiful, a delight to enjoy.

The emperor portraits by Yan Liben, and the fashionable *Qiluo* and Saddle Horse Characters displayed the newly found generosity and confidence of the great Tang Dynasty. In the *Imperial Palanquin*, we have discovered the grace, solemn and elegance of the imperial court and from the paintings of Zhang Xuan, Zhou Fang, Han Han and Han Guang, we have witnessed the affluent and opulent living standard of aristocracy in particular and the general public at large. All of these depict a golden age of economic prosperity and artistic creativity.

"The Painting Saga"

The most outstanding painter of the Tang Dynasty is Wu Daozi, and he is also considered by most collectors as the greatest talent of never known before and ever since. The great poem, Du Fu called him Painting Saga. *Famous Paintings Record of Past Dynasties* wrote: "Wu was walking on the time line of artistic achievement but he could not see Gu Kaizhi and Lu Tanwei in front of him and turning his head back no body was following." He was alone by himself. The great poet and painter of the Song Dynasty, Su Shi said, "for poets, you could not go beyond Du Zimei (Du Fu), for writers not beyond Han Yu, for calligrapher not beyond Yan Zhengqing and for painter not beyond Wu Daozi. All the developments from the past to the present completed without exception." Almost all the historic books on painting and its history have admired his achievement and agreed without exception that he is a "Painting Saga for hundred generations".

Wu Daozi (685–785 AD) was born in a poor family in Yu Xian of Henan Province. He started learning calligraphy from a young age and later turned his attention to painting. At age of twenty his talent started to shine. He went to the Capital Luoyang as amateur painter and soon afterwards, the Xuanzong emperor learnt his reputation and appointed him as a court scholar. The period Wu Daozi lived was a period during which the Tang Dynasty was at peak of its great prosperity and the Empire enjoyed an unprecedented economic power and artistic freedom and creativity. In the two capitals, Luoyang, the eastern capital and Chan'an the western capital, assembled the culture elites and the best, like twinkling stars brightening each other. *Famous Paintings Record of Past Dynasties* wrote: "up to now, the Tang Empire had enjoyed its prosperity for nearly two hundred thirty years, all the talents assembled and enriched each other and the most active was during the Kaiyuan and Tianbao periods of Xuanzong's reign," when the important Tang painters, Wu Daozi, Wang Wei, Zhang Zao, Li Sixun, Cao Ba, Han Gan, Chen Hong, Xiang Rong, Liang Lingzan, Zhang Xuan, and Yang Huizhi lived. They together with other numerous craft painters all competed for artistic creativity and during the process enriched each other and created a tremendous period of artistic variety and prosperity. Under the influence of this artistic environment and atmosphere, arrived Wu Daozi and he showed his magnificent talent and grew rapidly to his prominence. *Famous Paintings Record of Past Dynasties* wrote further and considered the Painting Saga with a near mythical dimension: "he was good at depicting characters of Taoism and Buddhism but he also showed great talents on other subjects such as *Shanshui*, birds and animals, grasses and plants, pavilions and pagodas, almost everything within his specialty."

He painted about four hundred or so murals of Buddhist subjects in temples around Luoyang and

"Fluttering Sleeves" and "Wet Clothing"
Tang-Dynasty painter Wu Daozi is renowned for his Buddha paintings with smooth strokes. Long sleeves in his paintings are fluttering as if they were blown up by the wind; therefore, "Fluttering Sleeves" has become a synonym of superb painting techniques and graceful styles, as well as a representational technique for sleeves. As opposed to "Fluttering Sleeves", "Wet Clothing" is a style of figure painting in which the clothing appears to be sticking to the bodies of the figures as if they have just come out of water. This style was originated by Cao Zhongda, a painter in the the Northern Qi Dynasty.

A copy of Wu Daozi's painting.

Chan'an, each of them was unique with its own characteristics and had emphasis of different features. Circle of light above Buddha, pillars and beams, arches and frames were all drawn with a single stroke and without aids of ruler and compass. His unique orchid branch and Brasenia leave looking like wrinkled dresses appeared to carry gentle breezes across and this style and method of painting was given a special name, "wind of Wu." He often painted spontaneously in pubic at Xing Shan Temple of Chan'an and the people of Chan'an would swarm to visit the temple on such an occasion, to see the master in action, practicing his signature one stroke spontaneous technique and to cheer creation of masterpieces unfolding in front of their eyes. Wu Daozi was also often using meticulous method of painting to decorate palaces and temples like craft painters and became a master of the artistic principle of "following the rhythm and perfecting each one." Consequently he was not only regarded by the culture elite as the Painting Saga but also considered by the craft painters and decorators as their founding grand master.

Wu Daozi had a great enthusiasm and pursued vigorously in the world of arts, very much like Michelangelo during the

Renaissance. *Famous Paintings Record of Past Dynasties* wrote: "when Wu Daozi painting, his arches like blades, his lines like pillars and beams, all without the help of rulers and compasses." When he doing figures, however large, he could start with either hands and arms or legs and foots, still being able to balance and control the overall composition. With the combination of meticulousness of a calligraphy and creativity of a great imagination, he painted many vivid pictures of beyond comparison, full of rhythm and colorful magic. His paintings did not deliberately exaggerate the flash of the heaven and the horror of the hell, and his inspiration mainly came from his thorough observation of earthly reality. His bold and unconstrained style of painting formed a remarkable contrast to the grace and elegance style of his predecessors Gu Kaizhi. However there is a common feature linked them two together, in which they both imitated the principle of calligraphy, in particular, the exquisite use of pen and the attention to the overall composition. Wu Daozi had been trained as a craft painter, and he was also a student of the great Tang calligraphers, Zhang Xu (date of birth unknown but he was most active during the reign of Xuangzong) and He Zhizhang (about 659–744 AD). He was especially fond of demented *caoshu* style (a rapid cursive writing style of calligraphy) and his paintings radiated with vibrant *caoshu* rhythm of "writings".

Wu Daozi almost spent his entire life devoted to the murals of religious matters, including paintings depicting Buddhism and Taoism teachings. For example, on the north corridor of western pagoda at Qianfu Temple, he created a Buddhisattva in his own image. Thereafter, Han Gan did the same in his religious murals, *Prostitute Xiao Xiao Writing on Chastity* and *A Column of Masters*. They tried symbolically to break the restraints of strict religious teachings and to be creative in a divine world. He would not like to act as the guardian of religion but as an ordinary painter to be able to enjoy the free spirit of artistic expression. He even brought the aristocrats into *the Hell: a Teaching Illustration*. Wu was also a very successful landscape painter. Once the Xuanzong emperor

Mural, cave 103 of Mogao Caves, carved in the heyday of the Tang Dynasty, a vivid description of Vimalakirti.

consigned him to go to Sichuan to study the sights and views of local importance and specifically asked to bring back sketches of places he visited so he could paint them on his return. He returned from his assignment but without a single sketch. The Xuanzong emperor was very disappointed and annoyed by his carefullessness. However he came to the court calmly without any fear and worry and painted without any hesitation. Before the eyes of Emperor and his court officials, hundred miles of the roaring Jialin River and vast land of exuberant Sichuan appeared in a lightening speed. He finished the whole painting within one day. The court was astonished.

The religious paintings during the Tang Dynasty followed the traditions of many Dynasties before it, among which the "Cao Family Style" was the most popular one, a style founded by Cao Zhongda (date of birth unknown and his active career period was from 550–577 AD). His style of Buddhist painting was a local transformation of the original Buddhist painting formula. It depicted anatomy of close fit dressed figures. It was called a special name "Cao dress out of water". During his early years, Wu Daozi often used delicate lines and a compact and concise style to paint. During his middle age he adopted a more muscular and free way of expression, often using stronger but mellow lines of alternative fine and heavy strokes and full of vibrancy, his signature Brasenia leave lines. There were often broken spaces in between his strokes, depicting a sense of broken lines but continuous rhythm. Together with another painter Zhang Sengyao, they collectively created the so called "Shuti (the loose style)", in contrast to the "Miti (the tight style)" of Gu Kaizhi and Lu Tangwei. Wu Daozi also distanced himself from the "Cao Family Style" of religious painting, and marked the beginning of a local approach. During the Six Dynasties, Sui and early Tang period, it was the Cao Family style dominated the field while after the Tang Dynasty reached its peak of great prosperity, the local born religious painting style of Wu had assumed its dominance.

Wu Daozi was a very prolific painter and there are ninety three painting collected in *Xuanhe Collection of Paintings*, including, *Presentation of Seal to the Emperor, Zhong Kui with Ten Fingers, Peacock and Ming Emperor, Celestial King with Pagoda, the God Guardian of Buddhism Scripts*. Among them, *Celestial King Delivering a Son*, is his most important painting, depicting the story of the birth of Shakyamuni Buddha, the son of King Shuddhadana, and is now in Osaka Municipal Museum of Art. The Portrait of Buddha is now in Toufuku temple, Kyoto Japan. Both of them are considered to be copies in his name only. His other important work, *Daozi Book of Scroll Paintings*, is a collection of ink and brush sketches painted

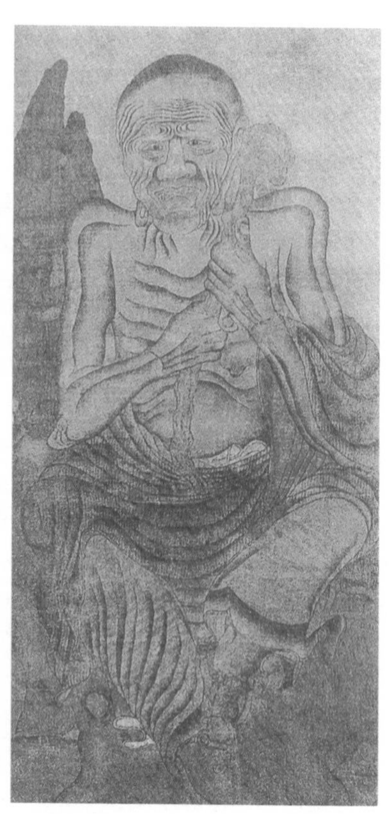

Sixteen Arhats (part), by Guan Xiu of the Tang Dynasties period.

on paper and it is believed 50 pieces remained today but it was smuggled out of China in 1911 and lost from general public ever since. Today we are only able to see its photocopies. Many of the so called original paintings by Wu Daozi today are actually copies done by the generations of painters after his death. These copies are although much less valuable than his original paintings but they are important references to study the style and a technique of Wu's painting. Those originals are gone forever and these copies should be treasured, as they are the only testimonial to a painter Saga.

Celestial King Delivering a Son, also called the Birth of Shakyamuni Buddha, has been a favourite item treasured by connoisseurs of many generations. It was a masterpiece ever painted. The painting was based on the Buddhist teaching, telling the story of the birth of Shakyamuni to the family of King Shuddhadana. The front section of the painting depicts a celestial being riding on an auspicious animal delivering a baby forward, the celestial king sitting upright, showing a very happy and anxious expression for he had just completed a very important task. All the court ladies and servants around him have expressed a very similar anxiety. The latter section of the painting illustrates the king Shuddhadana carries the baby Buddha gently, walking slowly forward with all the respects and gracefulness. *Daozi Book of Scroll Paintings* depicts many Taoist gods of the Earth and their associate celestial beings. In his paintings they are walking above clouds and the celestial court provides an atmosphere that they are in the heaven. However all celestial beings in these paintings have the images of ordinary people of the Tang period. Many of them have described the ghastly tragedy and punishment of hell in a format of Buddhist teaching illustration, depicting heaven and hell, by coincidence very similar to the scenes of Satan and purgatory in epic poems of Renaissance in Europe.

Famous Paintings Record of Past Dynasties (Li-dai ming-hua ji)

The Tang Dynasty presided a period of more than several hundreds of years,during which China enjoyed a great prosperity and the art world experienced a tremendous progress and advancement. Many paintings in this period achieved an artistic significance which was never accomplished before and after. As a consequence, many works published to study these paintings of historic significance. The earliest book on the Chinese painting history, *Famous Paintings Record of Past Dynasties,* was published during the late Tang Dynasty by Zhang Yanyuan. Zhang Yanyuan's great grand father, grand father, and father all served as prime ministers to the Tang Dynasty. His household collected my paintings of the Six Dynasties, Sui Dynasty and Tang Dynasty. *Famous Paintings Record of Past Dynasties* is considered to be the founding history book of Chinese paintings. Other important works on painting and its history during the Tang Dynast includes *Famous Paintings Records of the Tang Dynasty*, by Zhu Jingxuan (date of birth unknown and active career period from 806 to 835 AD) and *On Shangshui* and *On the Methods of Shanshui* by Wang Wei.

Famous Paintings Record of Past Dynasties by Zhang Yanyuan consists of ten volumes and three sections. The first section is on history of painting, the second is biographies of painters, and the third is collections of paintings of all Dynasties. The book has dealt with all the important issues associated with Chinese paintings, beginning with its origin and its social functions. The main body lists the names of important painters, all together 372 of them from Xuan Yuan to the Tang Huichang dynesty period. It is not only a book on the history of Chinese painting but also a collection of comments of painting critics, citing tens of previous works on painting history and painting theory. It is a comprehensive review and record up to the Tang Dynasty. It is a compulsive reading for all those who are interested in Chinese paintings.

Desert Treasures

Buddhism Going East

Buddhism and its associated arts were originated in Indian and spread mainly through two routes. It traveled to the central Asia, China, Korea and Japan through the northern route and to the Southeast Asia through the southern route. It syncretized with local characteristics in each of the places it reached during the journey eastward. It arrived in China in the 2nd Century AD and during the reign of the Eastern Han Dynasty. Wei Chronicles on Buddhism and Taoism wrote: "since the building of White Horse Temple in Luoyang, mural portraits of Buddha flourished in the country; all painted meticulously and adopted a universal formula." It went further: the Mingdi of the Han Dynasty ordered portraits of Buddha painted and displayed in Qingliang Pagoda and Xianjie Imperial Tomb. It shows that Buddhist arts had as long a history as Buddhism teaching itself in China. Buddhism and its associated

Statue of Musicians in Longmen Caves.

Statue of *Lushena* Buddha, Feng Xian Temple, Longmen Caves, height 17.14 m.

arts are very important and influential sources to the development of arts in China, only second to the traditional Chinese philosophic wisdom and teachings.

The development and progression of Buddhist arts were primarily subject to the demand of its religious believing

< Cave 12 of Yungang Caves, the "Music Cave", scenes of music festival to celebrate the enlightenment of Sakymuni.

and two of the most important characteristics of Buddhism were the worship of Buddha's image and the confirmation of protocols. The Buddhist arts developed in line with these traditions in order to help the preaching of teaching scripts and to assist the living in groups practiced by monks. The Buddha's sculpture was one of the most important aspects in Buddhism and in China it was often called the religion of Buddha's Sculptures. The religious paintings were mainly created to display the image of Buddha and to illustrate the Buddhist's teachings, such as birth of Buddha, legend of reincarnation and penance and enlightenment. At the beginning, Buddhism was a practical religion and did not appreciate the importance of sculptures and images. Since the death of Buddha Shakyamuni, believers started to worship his relics and processions, specially the tooth, after his cremation. They began to build pagodas to store these relics and painted murals and created sculptures to worship his teachings. The tradition of sculpture and image worship proceeded in earnest from then on.

Cave murals by and large have symbolized the Buddhist arts in China. Shanxian Caves and Kizil Caves in Xinjiang are perhaps the earliest caves carved in the third century AD. Mogao Caves or caves of thousand Buddha in Dunhuang are the most representative of large scale group caves survived. Mogao Caves have played a very important role to transform Buddhist arts from that of the religion of its birth place to that of the religion of China. It has been also an important interjection in the culture exchange between China and the outside world to its west. It has influenced and helped the proliferation of Buddhist cave arts to the other parts of the country.

Bian Xiang

"Bian Xiang", or simply *"Bian"*, refers to pictorial or carving illustrations of the sutras. It primarily depicts three kinds of scenes: first, the activities of the supreme and its attendants in their occupied area (the Pure Land), often known as "Configuration", for example, "the Configuration of the Pure Land of the West"; second, single or serial paintings recounting the life of the Buddha according to the biography of Sakyamuni, often known as "the Legend of the Buddha"; and third, single or serial paintings themed around the classics in the tale of Jataka (prior to the birth of Prince Sakya, often known as *"Jataka"*.

Murals on the top of cave 10 of Yungang Caves, *Fairies Going to Heaven*.

< Cave 259 of Dunhuang Mogao Caves, carved between 384 and 534 AD. Most statues are colored portraits of Buddha, fine example of the early period of Mogao cave arts.

Cave 20 of Yungang Caves, statue of sitting Sakymuni, height 13.7 m.

Other important sites of mural caves in China include: Bingling Temple Caves, and Maijishan Caves in Gansu province, Yungang Caves and Tianlong Mountain Caves in Shanxi province, Longmen Caves and Gongxian Caves in Henan province, Xiangtangshan Caves in Hebei province, Dazu Caves in Sichuan province and Jianchuan Caves in Yunnan province.

Zhang Yanyuan wrote in his *Famous Paintings Record of Past Dynasties.*

that many important painters in the Wei and Jin Dynasties and Tang Dynasty, including Cao Zhongda, Gu Kaizhi, Lu Tangwei (?–485 AD), Zhang Sengyao (date of birth unknown, and active career period from 502–549 AD), and Wu Daozi were also famous for their achievements in painting Buddhist subjects. The practice of the art not only provided a stage for them to perform and to arise to their fames but also enriched their artistic imaginations. During the late period of the Wei and Jin Dynasties, Zhang Sengyao was the most influential painter on Buddhist paintings. Again *Famous Paintings Record of Past Dynasties.*

commented on his technique: "one or two strokes, image appeared; from what was available create what was almost impossible; accurate portraits and unprecedented achievement; precise features and communicating rhythms." Before the Sui and Tang Dynasties, he was one of the most important pioneers and keen promoters of the newly arrived art form. Cao Zhongda however created his own style of religious painting, the "Cao Family Style", which was one of the four important schools of religious painting techniques. The paintings and sculptures during the Wei and Jin periods had a very similar artistic style to that of Indian Gupta Dynasty. Characters always wore close fit dresses showing full body features. This and the "Wu Family Style" of Wu Daozi were the two most important approaches of Buddhist paintings in China. Their techniques could be characterised into a simple term, "Cao family style is like a character wearing silk dress arising out of water and Wu family style is like with a silk ribbon flying with breeze." Unfornuately, most of works by Cao Zhongda has not survived and one rare sculpture of Buddha Shyakmuni collected by Luye Garden has his signature wet dress style. The Wu family style has a looser fit dress code, sleeves and ribbons moving with gentle wind like a celestial being of Chinese legend. His style can often be seen on the murals in Dunhuang.

The localization of Buddhist arts in China took a long period of time and did not complete until the Sui and Tang Dynasties. Most of the important art works however were completed during this transformation process and by the end of the great Tang Dynasty, the format and spirit eventually achieved unification and the Buddhist art became truly Chinese. It is worthwhile to mention

(left) A silk scroll of Mother Buddha, unearthed from the cave of Buddhist manuscripts at Dunhuang Mogao Caves, collected by the Guimet Museum, Paris.
(right) A silk scroll of Bodhisattva, unearthed from the cave of Buddhist manuscripts at Dunhuang Mogao Caves, collected by the Guimet Museum, Paris.

that some of the most important Buddhist art works in China were finished before the Sui and Tang Dynasties.

Buddhism arrived and flourished in China during the Eastern Han, and Wei and Jin Dynasties when China had a period of instability of wars and divisions. Dynasties came and went without effective control and authority. People, living in turmoil and chaos, lost their faith in a decadent ruling class and the society lost their faith in the traditional Chinese philosophical teachings, the Confucianism. Metaphysics tried to fill the spiritual vacuum and once became the fashion of society. Ideologically it is one of the most active periods in the Chinese history. Under this background Buddhism arrived and soon it gained tremendous popularity and fanatic convictions. From the north to south, the whole country

was constructing religious buildings, creating tens of thousands of temples, pagodas, towers, and caves. During the Northern Wei period (386–534 AD), the ruling class installed Buddhism as the religion of the state. From the Emperor, court officials to the ordinary people on the street, there were remarkable enthusiasms towards this newly arrived religion. Most of the important caves in China were made during this period, including Bingling Caves, Yungang Caves, and Maijishan Caves together with majority of the sculptures and murals. The major parts of Mogao Caves in Dunhuang, including the colored chapters, were also completed during this period. Therefore the north Wei Dynasty had registered a similar period of achievements and accomplishments of Buddhist arts as the great Tang Dynasty. The paintings and sculptures during this period were mainly depicting legends and life stories of Buddha and Bodhisattvas, emphasizing penance and enduring hardship to seek enlightenment. Murals and sculptures were often constructed to compliment each other in order to create a mutual harmony. Profiles are simple and elegant, having many of the original Indian features of Buddhist arts with succinct geometry. Today this school of artistic expression still has modern followers and admirers.

The simplicity and sincerity of the North Wei Dynasty were gradually replaced by the lavishness and elegance of the Tang Dynasty. Many elements of the original Indian Buddhist arts were disappearing and the localization of Buddhist images was taking place quietly but very steadily, a return of the national confidence and a rediscovery of the traditional Confucianism. During the Tang Dynasty of great prosperity, the economic power and the national confidence reached an unprecedented height. The combination of this national reality and the inspired artistic imagination provided a perfect setting for many magnificent projects of arts. The scale, the enthusiasm and the order, by which these projects were executed, were beyond imagination. The contents of murals during this period are mainly related to the *Western Paradise of Amitabha*

Buddhist manuscript scroll unearthed from Dunhuang Caves, collected by National Library of France.

and *Dharmmapada Scripts*, depicting the celestial abundance of the western paradise, a Buddhist utopian ideal. Illustration to teach Buddhist scripts is main topics for most murals of the Tang Dynasty. The main characteristic of the Chinese localization is the addition of elements of ordinary daily life. The composition of murals that period are therefore often solemn, lavish, majestic and grand but at the same time full of secular delights and details of daily life. The portraits of Yan Liben, the *Qiluo* Characters of Zhang Xuan and others and the paintings by Wu Daozi, all have defined major characteristics of paintings during the Tang Dynasty, many of which can also be found on murals of the same period. Spiritual Buddha and Bodhisattvas have been created out of the same molds to secular Emperors and court ladies. Many of the scenes depicted in the illustration murals are aesthetic idealization and poeticization of daily reality.

In comparison to the simplistic and bold but unsophisticated expressions of the North and South periods, the techniques used

Buddhist manuscript scroll unearthed from Dunhuang Caves, collected by National Library of France.

on the illustration murals in the Tang period are more refined and full of artistic imaginations. Many are learnt from their noble counterparts of court officials and imperial painters. Even some of the royal painters had directly participated in many of the religious projects themselves, brought in with them the cultured perspectives and techniques. Maijishan and Mogao Cave murals have exemplified those of the Sui and Tang period. The colors are normally lucid and full of variety and variation. The compositions are heavy and complicated. The characters are modeled from court officials and ladies of that period, dignified and gracious and with characteristics of luxurious living. The musicians and music instruments displayed in front of Bodhisattvas are more extravagant than those murals in Ajanta of Indian. The Seven Pagoda, flowers and musicians, lotus ponds and trees and birds in the western paradise of Amitabha are fantasy of a luxurious and lavish living of celestial abundance, in sharp contrast to and clear deviation form the attitude of strict penance to seek the

A silk scroll of Tang period, unearthed from Dunhuang Caves, Bodhisattva guiding a dead woman to heaven.

enlightenment. All the Buddha, Bodhisattvas, and other celestial beings have a full sturdy figure, with colorful cheeks and full of grace and elegance, a reflection of the fashionable aesthetic standard of the Tang Dynasty. The mural creators have showed us a magnificent ability to control complicated scenes and to balance colossal magnitude of painting compositions. They skillfully used positions of palatial pavilions and mansions to manipulate depth of composition and exploited shade of colors and width and variety of lines to feature different characters, and also applied lucid and exuberant details and delights of secular daily life to enrich and humanise a celestial paradise.

The enthusiasm to depict the pure land of the western paradise lead to the creation of many magnificent and beautiful religious pictures of celestial world and normal life and pushed the mural paintings to a unprecedented level of sophistication. When the fantasy pushed too high reality would hit ground. Excess aestheticism and over indulgence finally broke the essence and spirit of the religious paintings. Many murals became a form without substances. As the localization of Buddhist arts progressed further, some artists went back to the traditional root of simplicity and sincerity and othes went further to paint more ostensible religious paintings without any essence. Perhaps it is not a surprise that after their heyday in the Tang Dynasty, Buddhist arts represented by murals and sculptures went into decline quickly during the Song Dynasty which followed.

Dunhuang Mogao Caves

Mogao Caves are built on the cliffs between Mingshao Mountain and Sanwei Mountain to the southeast of Dunhuang, 1618 meters long in the direction from the south to the north. The building and carving started in 366 AD and lasted for about one thousand years. All the dynasties during the one thousand years history participated in the building of the caves and the most active period is the Tang Dynasty. There are 45000 square meters of murals and 2000 colored sculptures survived. They are the largest and best preserved collections of Buddhist cave arts and treasures in the world. Because Dunhuang was in a strategic point on the traditional Silk Road on the west frontier of China, it was an important junction for the exchange of people and culture between China and the western regions (xiyu).

The Dunhuang Mogao Cave treasures include architectures, color sculptures, murals and as well as books and record. Its architectures, murals and sculptures have symbolized the Buddhist arts of China as three integrated parts. The colored sculptures and murals in the north Wei and west Wei periods (535–556 AD) exemplify the highest achievement of early period of Dunhuang arts. There are 36 caves belonged to this period. Murals are painted around on all walls and ceiling as well as pillars supporting ceilings. Apart from a few decorative paintings most are to illustrate Buddhist legend stories and the birth of Buddha, and the cause and predestined relationship. There are many images of Bodhisattvas, figures of celestial beings and pictures of musicians and dancers. For example, *Prince Sattva Feeds Himself to the Hungry Tigress* in cave 254, *Conversion of the 500 Robbers* in cave 285, *Buddha's Preaching* in cave 249, *The Nine-colored Deer Saves the Drowning Man* in cave 257 and *The Buddha's Life Stories* in cave 290 are all delicately painted with magnificent and rigorous compositions, masterpieces of very high artistic value and great historic achievement.

The murals of Dunhuang of this period have still kept many original elements of Buddhist arts in terms of subjects portrayed and painting methods adopted. The Buddha's Life and Jataka stories are all directly from the Buddhist teaching classics. Similar murals and subjects are also found in caves in Indian. During this early stage of mural arts in China, the images and features from a foreign land were still kept unchanged as they were viewed as representatives of gods and accepted as the spiritual essence of Buddhism. For example, the half naked images of Buddha and various gods are prominently portrayed on these murals. Actually all symbolic postures have followed and copied their original Indian formulas. The "Indian coloring method" of using dark and light shades to depict a sense of three dimensional effects is another direct example that traditional Indian painting method has been adopted. The traditional postures and the images of half nakedness were regarded as essential part of Buddhist teachings and therefore were directly portrayed without any modification. However, the more trivial details in murals were more or less left to the imagination of individual painters who could paint according to their own experience. For example, most of the hunting scenes are very much like the traditional Chinese paintings. They were consciously or unconsciously changing the more perceptual elements of Buddhist murals such as clothing and body features. Musicians, celestial beings, and minor Bodhisattvas had become half Chinese and half Indian. But in overall, the will to add true realism into the more conceptual composition of Buddhist murals were inhibited during the north Wei period because of the earnest respect and tremendous admiration for the religion of the foreign land. Consequently the mural figures of that period are very bold and unconstrained, and very conceptual and colors are generally very lucid. The overall effect is very decorative.

There are many scenes of entertainment and performance, banqueting and drinking, and as well as playing games and matches on the murals in Ajanta caves in Indian. All the Bodhisattvas are dressed lavishly with variety of postures and lucid colors. Even constraining and defeating devils look like a stage setting without any elements of horror and fear.

Dunhuang Frescos

The internationally acclaimed Dunhuang No. I Cave was first built in 366 AD. The frescos and color figurines in Dunhuang's early caves were heavily influenced by India and Central Asia; "the unique Dunhuang style" was not formed until the Northern Wei Dynasty; and the influence of the Central Plains culture was the most significant in the Western Wei Dynasty. Works from this era mostly depict the localized tales of Jataka and Buddhist monks and nuns; subjects from India and Central Asia are often uniquely integrated with Chinese themes and styles in the same cave, as evidenced by Cave 249 which was built in the final years of the Northern Wei Dynasty. In this particular cave, the frontal Buddha sculpture is flanked by Bodhisattva and Apsaras and surrounded by many smaller Buddha sculptures, known as "the Thousand Buddha". The color-painted niche for Buddha above the frontal Buddha sculpture depicts musical Apsaras playing various instruments. Representative Dunhuang caves include Cave 275 (from the Sixteen Kingdoms Period), Cave 257 (from the Northern Wei Dynasty), Cave 254 (also from the Northern Wei Dynasty), Cave 428 (from the Northern Zhou Dynasty), and Cave 285 (from the Western Wei Dynasty).

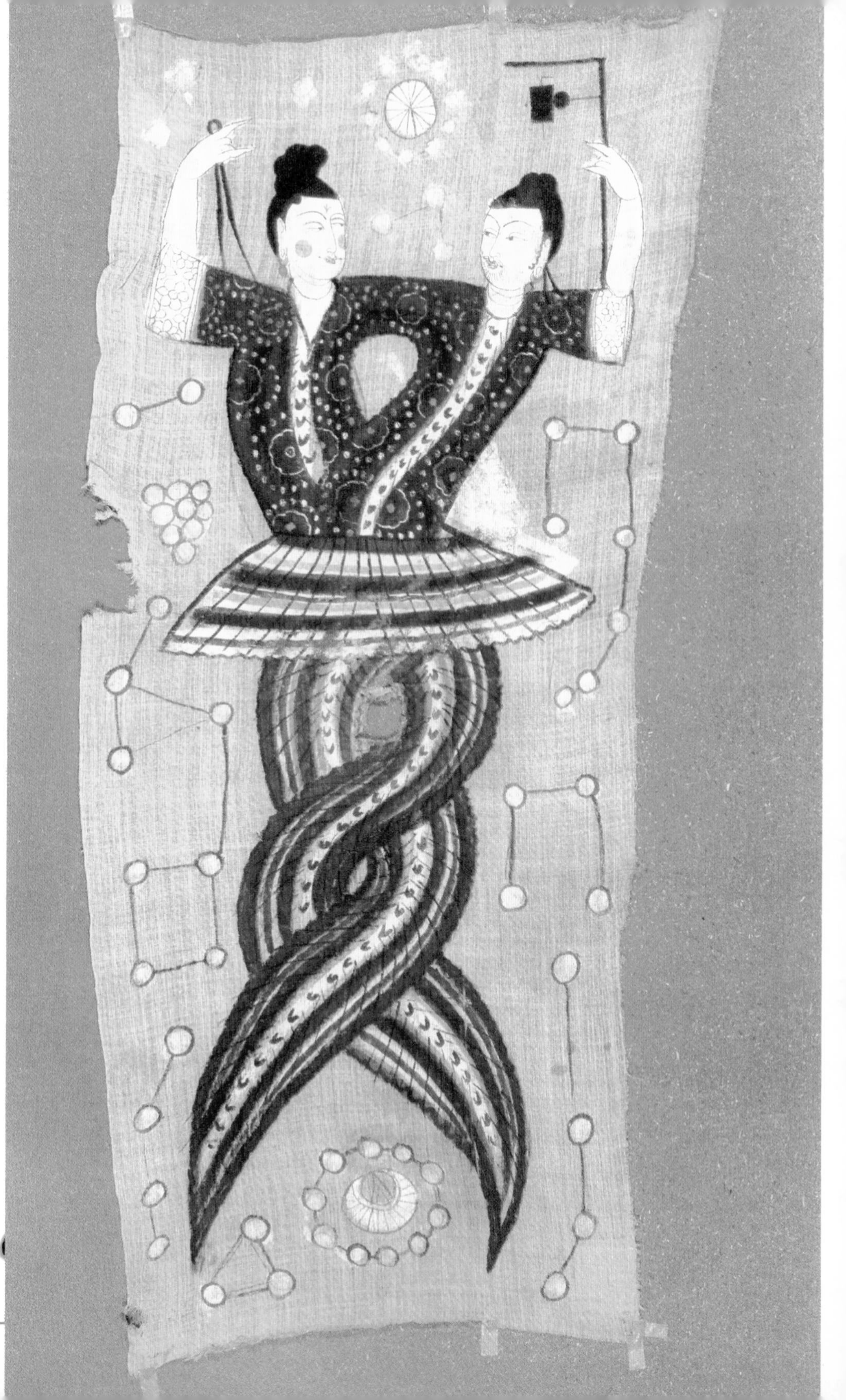

In contrast, murals in the north Wei period are more frightening and ghastly in depicting subjects of this type, such as penance, feeding tigers, and robbers taking eyes. The composition and colors are though still bold and unconstrained without a sense of gentleness and loveliness.

Shivering burning fires depicted on the murals in caves 249 and 257 of Mogao are radiated with blazing enthusiasm, which seemly reminds us of the gothic style of Christian paintings. In effect, they were an extension of ancient Chinese silk and brick plate paintings in the Han period which could also be seen in the paintings of Gǔ Kaizhi. Similarly the portrayals of Bodhisattvas, Buddha, and celestial beings appear to be like Saints and angels in Christian teachings. However a closer examination would reveal that they are the combination of Indian figures with Chinese elements of depicting celestial beings such as silk dresses and ribbons and spreading flower pedals in celestial heaven. The use of these elements has added more vivid and lucid as well as mystic images to a rather sincere and plain subject. Several *Hunting* murals and *The Nine-colored Deer Saves the Drowning Man* have combined again the Buddhist story with the scenes of brick plate paintings in the Han period, an imaginative and symbolic expression of people and animals, appropriate to convey the implicit meaning in the

(left) Cave 423 of Dunhuang Mogao Caves, carved during the Sui period, apart for the murals, a significant item is the Inscriptions of *"on Mogao Caves"*.
(right) *Sutra of the Buddha of Infinite Life,* mural, cave 217 of Dunhuang Mogao Caves, carved during the heyday of the Tang Dynasty.

< *Fuxi and Nvwu* silk scroll, unearthed from the cave of Buddhist manuscripts, Dunhuang Mogao Caves, collected by the Guimet Museum, Paris.

Buddhist story. Mountains and trees on background are created using local abundantly available red clay with the addition of other heavy colors, a technique often used in gold and silver art wares and on murals of tomb chambers during the Han period.

On the mural *Illustration of Defeating the Evil King* in cave 254, Shakyamuni is sitting solemnly and sincerely in the middle and on his two sides stand the evil king, his three evil beauties and other demons, depicting Buddha avoiding the temptation of beauty and defeating the force of evil. Soon the evil king lost all his plots and fell to the ground, and his three beauty demons also revealed their true bodies of three old women. The earth was trembling and mountains were quaking. Heads of other demons appeared falling form their shoulders and running away as quickly as they could. The story is told in one single mural and it has adopted a relatively simple and plain style, mainly relying on the contrast created by trembling earth and quaking mountains and the violent demons

Murals, cave 296 of Dunhuang Mogao Caves, painted 557 to 581 AD, top and low layers, depicting the busy trade route of "silk road."

to depict the solemn and serene of Shakyamuni. The mural is full of strong religious teachings and scenes of terror as if the painter had temporarily lost his sanity, disregarding conventional and secular aesthetic standard. The murals in the north Wei period have carried more foreign elements than any other ancient Chinese arts and this trend would only be rectified during the forthcoming Sui and Tang periods.

A colored statues of the Tang period in cave 194 of Dunhuang Mogao Caves, most Buddhas with chubby cheeks and plump body, and very lightly dressed, a reflection of aesthetic standard of the period.

The Mogao murals of the Sui and Tang periods are more concentrated on the Purification of the Buddha-Field, teaching illustration of Buddhist scripts, and portraits of Buddha and Bodhisattvas, an obvious deviation from the more common topics of sacrifice, penance, liberation and the Jataka Stories. There are much richer contents and more lucid colors. The horizons of expression are also significantly extended. Since the western paradise was a fashionable concept during that period, there are about 228 murals, depicting the Purification of the Buddha-Field. Even other topics for example *Musicians on the Pure Land*, and *Paying a Debt of Gratitude*, also have adopted the western paradise as main background. There are 207 mural caves in Mogao carved during the Tang Dynasty, which is normally divided into four periods, the early, the great, the middle and the late Tang. For example cave 220 was built in the early Tang in the 16th year of Zhenguang period (642 AD), cave 335 was built during the great Tang in the 2nd year of Chuihong period (686 AD), and cave 130 and cave 172 also built in the great Tang during the Kaiyaung and Tianbao periods. Cave 112 was built in the middle Tang and cave 156 built in the late Tang. All these caves have hosted many magnificent works and they are the most representative of Buddhist arts in the

Silk painting of *the Amitabha,* unearthed from Dunhuang Mogao Caves, collected by the British Museum.

A colored statue of Bodhisattva, cave 384 of Dunhuang Mogao Caves, carved in the heyday of the Tang Dynasty.

Tang period.

The main characters on murals of the Sui and Tang periods had eventually deviated from bold symbolic representation of images, a tradition of the north Wei period and started to show full facial features. For example, *the Bodhisattva Portrait* in cave 103 have the usual grace and elegance associated with traditional benevolent characters of Chinese paintings with little trace of foreign elements and their facial and body features and clothing are all very characteristic of Chinese. Court ladies on the murals in cave 285 look very similar to those on the paintings of Gu Kaizhi. The portraits of emperors in cave 220 are almost exact copies of *the Thirteen Emperors* of Yan Liben. The lavishness and exuberance shown on western paradises on the murals has depicted utopia of the Promised Land in Buddhist teaching but the subjects illustrated has more earthly elements and origins. For example, hunting, banqueting, carriage, boating, theatre, performance, cultivation, farm animals, commence, medical treatment are all modelled on real life during the Tang period. Many murals also have landscape as background. Art historians often consider that the Tang Dynasty is the period when Chinese landscape painting finally became an independent genre. However, there are very few works of landscape from that period survived. Therefore landscape on the murals of the same period has became a very important source material to study its development during the Tang Dynasty. Many mural shanshuis of that period still have had elements of wildness, with exuberant mountains and sharp cliffs, decorated with pine forests and waterfalls, here and there showing some vibrant running wild animals.

Caves 158, 159, 217 and 220 have portrayed a similar subject, *the Western Paradise of Amitabha*. Amitabha is the Buddha presiding over the Western Paradise. He is sitting on a lotus throne at the center of the paradise. By his side are the Bodhisattva Avalokiteshvara and the historical Buddha along with other bodhisattvas. In front of the throne there are many dancers and other artists, dancing either in pairs or in singles with musicians playing the instruments on each of their sides. The composition is structured around a pond at the center and a series of palatial mansions at the back, with golden and silver floors and colored glazes mirrored reflection of lucid lights. Children are playing in the pond and lotus is in full blossom. Celestial court ladies are spreading flower petals. It is a total extravagance of abundance. Amitabha is sitting there sincere and tranquil with grace and elegance.

People in the Tang Dynasty admired the enjoyment of extravagance and lavishness, in a sharp contrast to the Buddhist teachings of sacrifice and penance. Murals of Buddhist illustrations in the Tang period tried to teach the traditional concepts of Buddhism, for example, those murals illustrated *the Saddharmapundarika Sutra. The Saddharmapundarika Sutra* promotes the goal of total enlightenment and in order to achieve this goal, one has to endure a life long of suffering and hardship. Most ordinary people would not be able to go through this life long of hardship and suffering and would give up before reaching the final enlightenment. Therefore *the Saddharmapundarika Sutra* use the following story of city of mirage to teach people to go on until the final enlightenment. A group of people went to a far away place to seek for treasures and during its journey they had to overcome many obstacles and endure unimaginable sufferings. After a while, people were exhausted and lost their faith. They could not go any further and thought to turn around and to go back home. At this moment, a wise guardian produced a mirage city in front of them, all the palatial mansions and pavilions with gardens and rivers surrounding them. People were delighted and went into the town, thinking they had found the treasures and there was no need to travel further. After seeing people were so contempt, the wise guardian made the town disappeared and told people that the town was only a place for taking a rest not their final destination. They needed to continue their journey until they finally got their treasures. The murals in cave 217 rebuild the town of mirage with vivid imagination of artists, depicting a lucid and broad landscape painting full of the details of the story.

Group portraits of Bodhisattva in cave 285 of Dunhuang Mogao Caves, painted 535–556 AD.

The sponsors of mural projects are another important subject for the content of murals. The most famous example of this is the mural *Travelling* in cave

156. Zhang Yichao was the highest ranking political official in the northwest region where Dunhuang belonged to. The *Travelling* depicts the story of a hunting trip Zhang Yichao took together with his family and their triumphed returning. Zhang is riding a red saddle horse and is accompanied by tow columns of knights on horse back on each of his side, with trumpets and drums played to their highest volumes, and many hunting dogs and Mongolian gazelles running backwards and forwards, a splendid hunting day out. On another mural *Song State Queen (the wife of Zhang Yichao) Going Out*, Zhang's wife rides on a bright white horse, accompanied by maids and servants and many dancers and musicians, traditional saddle horse characters of the Tang Dynasty, just like those in the paintings *the Shepherd Horse* and *Night-Shining White* of Han Gan. Also on the mural there are a group of magicians and some of them are trying to climb to an erected column, with a whole orchestra at background, a vivid description of a magnificent social event. It is very interesting to note that painters so delicately painted a mural of such extravagance and lavishness to commemorate its sponsor and to thank his support. This also illustrates an important social relationship during the Tang Dynasty and the characteristics of Buddhism believers. Murals in Mogao Caves have marked the completion of localization of Buddhist arts in China. They are also the results of ultimate unification of traditional Chinese painting techniques and the Buddhist teachings modified to suit the social and national characteristics. They have changed the bold and unconstrained conceptual style of the north Wei periods and enriched both the techniques and the compositions. The elegant use of lines and colors has balanced the grand and imposing magnificence with lucid and refreshing gentle details. The murals in cave 220 which were completed in the 16th year of Zhenguang period are the best kept murals in Dunhuang and illustrated the highest achievement of the Tang period.

Lucid Mountains and Remote Streams

Painting Academies in Song Dynasty
The Song Dynasty is the period of time where China's painting academies reached their apex. Painting academies in this particular period featured the most complete organizational form and comprehensive systems in art education in various aspects, such as discipline development and examinations. With a surging economy, the Northern and Southern Song Dynasties saw rapid development of painting academies, which would become the exemplary models for painting academies in subsequent dynasties. Emperor Huizong of Song, Zhao Ji, is credited with bringing painting academies to their pinnacle. He opened painting studies in the third year of the Chongning Reign (1104) and officially incorporated them into the scope of the imperial examinations to identify skilled painters. The painting studies were focused on six major subject matters, including Buddha, human figures, landscapes, birds and beasts, flowers and bamboos, and houses; and questions in the examinations were based on ancient poems and verses. Painters employed by the painting academy are divided into six ranks and treated nicely. *Xuanhe Collection of Painting*, which contained Song-Dynasty imperial panting and calligraphic works, remain important materials today for the study of China's ancient painting history.

Northern Painters and Southern Painters

In his book *Famous Paintings Record of Past Dynasties*, Zhang Yanyuan wrote, shanshui (Chinese landscape painting) was initiated by Wu Daozi and matured with Li Sixun (651–718 AD) and his son Li Zhaodao (birth and death years unknown). None of Wu's original paintings have survived, but several major original works of two Lis have endured the history of thousand years and are still available for us to enjoy. Li Sixun's *Sailing Boats and Pavilions* (*Jiangfan Louge Tu*) features tourists strolling by riverside, azure skies, boats on the misty river and exquisite buildings at the foot of hills, scenes that symbolize vastness and tranquility. The tree trunks, twigs and leaf veins are painted by using the "double outline technique." The rocks are outlined in vigorous strokes using the center portion of brush without obvious radiating faint inks on both sides of strokes. It is a technique of Zhan Ziqian, a Sui Dynasty painter. But the trees and rocks are drawn in great detail as if they were copies of nature. Main colors used are blue and green, but the turning points of ink lines are decorated with shining gold, a sharp contrast to its overall color tone. The painting embodies the lucidity and colorfulness exhibited in Zhan's *Spring Out* (*You Chun Tu*). Li Zhaodao further improved his father's style and reached a new level of sophistication. His *Journey in the Spring Mountain* (*Chunshan Xinglv Tu*) and *Emperor Xuanzong's Journey to Sichuan* (*Minghuang Xing Shu Tu*) are both painted on vertical silk scrolls with light colors. The paintings feature changing mists, remote

valleys, rushing waterfalls, lush forests and leisurely tourists on horsebacks. Despite the small size of the scrolls, the grand composition of magnificent scenes is all vividly depicted.

The "outline technique" means to draw the contour of the images with ink lines. Usually two strokes, either side by side or one above another, are drawn, merging in centre. Then transparent colors are used to create a shade before brilliant, nontransparent mineral colors are applied. This approach is thus known as "double outline technique." It is a traditional painting technique. Before the Song Dynasty, painters from Gu Kaizhi to those during the heydays of the Tang Dynasty often employed this method in their landscape and figure paintings and paintings of flowers and birds. "Double outline" is also evident in Chinese calligraphy to imitate many important original works. After the Tang and Song dynasties, many painters devoted themselves to landscape. They used the main body or the side of brush to make strokes to imitate grains of rocks and veins of tree barks, an approach that is known as the "stroke technique." To depict grains of different rocks, several painters developed a number of highly individualistic stroke techniques, such as Hemp-Fiber Strokes of Juran, Straight Rubbing Strokes of Guang Tong and Li Cheng and Raindrop Strokes of Fan Kuan. Terms such as "hemp-fiber" and "raindrop" were first used by art critics to describe the respective characteristics of different stroke types and they have since been integrated into the terminology of Chinese painting.

The transition period between the Tang Dynasty and the Northern Song Dynasty is called the Five Dynasties (907–956 AD). It was in this brief period

Emperor Xuanzong's Journey to Sichuan (55.9cmx81cm), by Li Zhaodao, collected by Taipei Palace Museum.

Lushan Mountain (185.8cmx106.8cm), by Jing Hao, collected by Taipei Palace Museum.

that the status of landscape was defined. We live by nature. But for Chinese painters it also embodies the *dao* (the truth). The Northern School represented by Jing Hao and Guan Tong was famous for their grand composition of large mountains and broad rivers. However, the signature style of the Southern School represented by Dong Yuan and Juran is their simplistic depiction of southern China, a world of constant misty, drizzly rains and light breezes. Traditional "*blue and green shanshui*" declined in popularity. Scholar painters began to emphasize the use of brush and the application of ink. Ink-and-wash landscapes, without the use of colors or with only light colors, reached its maturity. Painters also began to explore the philosophical dimension of their paintings.

Jing Hao (birth and death years unknown), art name Haoran, was a native of Qinshui in today's Shanxi Province. He took retreat in the Honggu Valley of Taihang Mountain at the end of the Tang Dynasty and therefore called himself Honggu Zi. His paintings inherited the traditional brush and ink skills developed in the Tang Dynasty. *Lushan Mountain* (*Kuang Lu Tu*) is a painting recreated the breathtaking views of Lushan Mountain. The painting has a majestic but careful balanced composition and it used a combination of remote in depth and remote in horizon perspectives. It is a typical "panorama *shanshui*," as defined by the painters in the Song Dynasty. From the lands at the foot of maintain to the remote peaks, Jing emphasized the magnificence of remote peaks while focusing the details of front views. Separated and yet harmoniously together, mountains are vividly represented in a vertical scroll, which is regarded as a model for Chinese landscape painting. Viewing the scroll from bottom to top, you will find images divided into several distinct sections. On the bottom are trees, cottages, rivers, stone paths, men on boat and muleteers at the foot of the mountains. Further up are mountain peaks, waterfalls, pavilions, bridges, and forests in mists and clouds. Contrasted by surrounding mountains, the central peak appears high and precipitous, soaring into the sky. In the painting

Jing integrated organically the three methods of outlining, broad stroking and shading, thus highlighting its texture and composition and the three dimensional feel of the images while illustrating the special artistic charm of ink-and-wash painting.

Jing realized the careful use of ink could create a depth of colors. Clouds, mists and water streams drawn in thin lines had a more romantic and symbolic feel. This style of technique is evident in the paintings of Gu Kaizhi and Zhan Ziqian. Instead of thin lines, Jing began to use different shades of ink to depict mountain mists. He wrote, "Wu Daozi uses brush but not ink, whereas Xiang Rong uses ink but not brush. I will try to use both and, find a balance and create a style of its own." He made his ambition known. He aimed to identify the features of brush and ink skills and to maximize both of their values. As many more scholars participated in the art of painting, "precise brush and romantic ink" became a core criterion to judge paintings. During Jing's time, his approach of perfect balance of brush and ink was very practical. For example, while depicting a waterfall, the rigidness of lines and strokes could be softened using the depth of ink shades.

Guan Tong (date unknown) was born in Chang'an. When he was young, he learned from Jing Hao and during his later years he made higher achievements than Jing. He was respectfully entitled "chulan," meaning "better than his teacher." Together they were called "Jing-Guan" collectively. He often visited Qinling mountain and Huanshan mountain and his favorite painting compositions were mountains of autumn and forests of winter, and village rural life. He had a painting style of very simple strokes, but depicting a strong sense of purpose and meaning. His famous paintings include *Journey in Mountains* (*Guanshan Xinglv Tu*) and *Waiting for Boat at Mountain Stream* (*Shanxi Daidu Tu*). Both survived and are collected by Taipei Palace Museum. *Journey in Mountains* shows high mountains and deep valleys covered by clouds. In the mountains sits a small temple, on the front a small bridge and a guest house, and many tourists and traders, full of life and rural

Lucid Mountains and Remote Streams scroll (185.8cmx106.8cm), by Xia Gui, collected by Taipei Palace Museum.

Journey in Mountains (144.4cm×56.8cm), by Guan Tong, collected by Taipei Palace Museum.

Waiting for Boat at the Xiajingshan Pass scroll (50cm×320cm), ink and color on silk (part), by Dong Yuan, collected by Liaoning Museum.

freshness. The trees were painted with simple but strong strokes. *Waiting for Boat at Mountain Stream* also illustrates his style of depicting grand mountains and their magnificent power.

Dong Yuan of the Southern Painting Sect, art name Shuda, date of birth unknown, died in 962. He was born in Zhongling (present-day northwest of Jinxian, Jiangxi province). Most of his paints have sceneries of south of the Yangtze River with exuberant grasses and trees. He usually used thin and long moist strokes, which was called "hemp-fiber stroke." Sometimes, he also painted bushes and grasses with dots of inks. His painting *People of the Suburb of Longsu* (*Longsu Jiaomin Tu*), collected by Taipei Palace Museum, shows round mountains and thick grasses and trees. At the foot of the mountains, a family hangs lanterns on trees, a scene of a joyful festival. The characters in the painting were painted meticulously with heavy color while mountains and water were painted using hemp-fiber strokes. *A Summer Mountain* (*Xiashan Tu*) kept at Shanghai Museum, *Waiting for Boat at the Xiajingshan Pass* (*Xiajingshankou Daidu Tu*) by Liaoning Museum and XiaoXiang River (Xiaoxiang Tu) by Beijing Palace Museum, all illustrate his typical style of simple inks and harmony of shape and shade, mostly describing mountains of south China, a land of exuberant growth and a contrast view of misty and bright.

Mi Fu, calligrapher and art critic of the Northern Song Dynasty was an admirer of the simple and innocent style of Dong Yuan's paintings. Dong Yuan tried to reproduce what he saw. The southern China he lived however lacks precipitous cliffs and ridges of northern China. In his painting *XiaoXiang River*, he abandoned the use of color and there are no unusual mountain peaks and strong rocks. Instead, there are the vast river, the misty sky and a lofty view. On the river, small boats carrying people and fishermen throwing out fishnets. On the bank, people engaged in religious ceremony. Shen Kuo of the Song Dynasty commented on Dong Yuan's paintings, "strokes are few in his paintings. A close look they seem not to be what supposed to be. A view from the distance, they

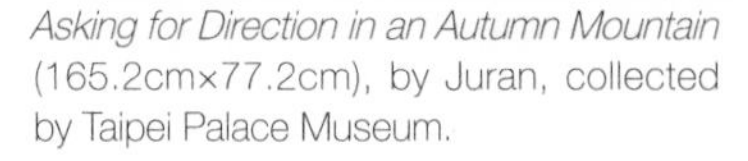
Asking for Direction in an Autumn Mountain (165.2cm×77.2cm), by Juran, collected by Taipei Palace Museum.

Whispering Pines in the Mountains (165.2cm×77.2cm), by Li Tang, collected by Taipei Palace Museum.

are a magnificent resemblance of what intended." His innocent and simplistic style and fact that the views need to be appreciated form a distance indicated his realistic intention. During the Han and Tang Dynasties, the grand painting style of north China was the mainstream of Chinese paining philosophy and practice. His realistic intention and attempt to depict true mountains and waters inevitably blew a fresh air into the dominance of the northern painters.

Juran (date unknown) was born in Jiangning (Nanjing) and was a Buddhist monk at Kaiyuan Temple in Jiangning and his active career continued even into the Northern Song Dynasty. He was a student of Dong Yuan, good at painting with simple ink and moist brushwork. The hemp-fiber strokes were his specialty. Many of his original works survived, including Asking for direction in a *Autumn Mountain* (*Qiushan Wendao Tu*) (Taipei Palace Museum), *Valleys and Pines Trees in Wind* (*Wanhe Songfeng Tu*) (Shanghai Museum), *Rocks and Bushes* (*Cengyan Congshu Tu*) (Taipei Palace

Museum), *Xiaoji Zhuanlanting Pavilion* (*Xiaoji Zhuanlanting Tu*) (Taipei Palace Museum) and *Buddhist Retreat by Stream and Mountain* (*Xishan Lanruo Tu*) (The Cleveland Museum of Art). Juran continued and further developed Dong Yuan's style of light ink and misty depiction. He explored the use of ink to its maximum effect and very often used watery ink to achieve his intended results.

During the Tang and Song Dynasties, Zen was popular in China and painters of Southern China advocated the spirit of flat and innocence. Dong Yuan and Juran's paintings, though mountains were high and grand, did not have a sense of magnificence. Mi Fu praised their paintings and wrote, "their paintings have a clear and moist scent, with innocent outlines," and "Juran's paintings with exuberant lands are full of life and freshness. Running mountains extended into the distance and on the valleys between them dotted with farm houses with doors open and a small path in front winding its way to the depth of the valleys. Trees lined in all directions, rocks standing in the middle of rivers beating waves against, and grasses dancing in the wind. As a Buddhist monk, Juran had an apathetic attitude to life more than Dong Yuan would, and thus, Juran's paintings had fewer and lonelier people and many deserted sceneries. His paintings made people feel more isolated from the society. The artist concerned more on the universe in his heart and mind and much less on the materialist world at large. The scholars in the generations followed admired Juran and treasured his paintings, mainly because they loved his Zen philosophy.

Painting history always associated Jing, Guan, Dong and Ju with the Five Dynasties and the early Northern Song Dynasty. They actually inherited and represented the highest level of sophistication of landscapes of both Northern and Southern China. They had a unique place in the history of landscapes. Northern China style had many followers in the North Song Dynasty and produced many masters. Because southern China style was promoted by scholars, they gained popularity in the Yuan Dynasty.

In the Ming and Qing Dynasties, whenever discussing landscape, Dong and Ju would be mentioned and the northern China style of "panorama *shanshui*" was gradually forgotten.

Song Huizong and his period

Following the achievements in the Sui, Tang and the Five Dynasties, further progress was made in the field of painting during the Song Dynasty. Imperial court painting, scholar-officials' painting and folk painting, each exhibiting distinct features yet keeping influencing, and infiltrating into others, jointly defined the painting of the Song Dynasty.

The Northern Song Dynasty unified the country, ending the turmoil caused by feudal states that tore the nation apart and ushering in a period of social stability. As commerce and the handicraft industry underwent rapid development, urban civilization flourished. Zhao Ji, the eighth emperor of the Northern Song Dynasty otherwise known as Huizong, went down in history for his political incompetence and obsession with art. When the Northern Song was overthrown by the Jin Dynasty of the northern nomads in 1127, emperor Huizong and his son Zhao Heng, or emperor Qinzong, were captured and jailed by the invaders and died miserably years later. After the fall of the Northern Song Dynasty, the imperial court retreated to the south where they established the Southern Song Dynasty (1127–1279) with Lin'an as the capital city. Immigrants from the north exploited the resourceful south and together with the locals created a period of sustained economic and cultural developments. Bianliang (Kaifeng, Henan province) and Lin'an (Hangzhou, Zhejiang province), respective capitals of the Northern Song Dynasty and the Southern Song Dynasty, were both prosperous commercial cities. Apart from aristocrats, the cities were home to large numbers of merchants, handicraftsmen and ordinary urban dwellers, boasting an extremely colorful cultural life. Painting was incorporated into

Plum Blossoms and a White-Eye (24.5cm×24.8cm), by Zhao Jie, collected by Beijing Palace Museum.

commerce and the handicraft industry, with painters selling their works in marketplaces. In the brisk fairs in Bianjing's Daxiangguo Temple held five times a month, there were stalls offering books and paintings. In the night market of Lin'an, painted fans were sold. Many restaurants in Bianjing, Lin'an and other cities were decorated with paintings to attract customers. When arranging banquets, urban residents could rent screens, hanging scrolls and calligraphy works to decorate. *Pictures of Door God and Zhong Kui* were tremendous popular at the end of year to cater for the needs of Spring Festival celebrations. As the handicraft industry made strides, block printing developed and became widely adopted, with Bianjing, Lin'an, Pingyang, Chengdu and Jianyang rising to

宿雨清畿甸
朝陽麗帝城
豐年人樂業
壠上踏歌行

become centers of the printing industry. Many books and Buddhist scriptures were illustrated. Printings of the Song and Jin period still available today such as Buddha portraits, Mantras of the Dharani Sutra, *Pictures and Eulogies of Sudhana's Journey to the South* (*Foguo Chanshi Wenzhu Zhinan Tuzan*) and *Zhaocheng Tripitaka* (*Zhaocheng Zang*) all feature exquisite craftsmanship.

Chinese painting peaked in the Song Dynasty. In the entire art history of ancient Chinese paintings, the paintings of the Song period had the most remarkable features of extensive depiction of the real life. The painters created many artistic techniques that were closely linked with the society in a variety of imposing styles. The painting styles, forms and theories in the later Yuan, Ming and Qing dynasties were all evident in the paintings of the Song Dynasty, a testament to the maturity and full flourish of the Chinese painting in that period. Many important breakthroughs in painting techniques were made in the Song Dynasty. Emphasis was laid on the human figures' emotions, intriguing plots and the creation of distinctively characterized images. Painters specializing in flowers, birds, mountains and rivers tried to produce a pleasant artistic conception, while stressing ingenious, true-to-life portrayal of the images. Scholar-official painters also played a positive role in boosting the art of painting, with remarkable contributions to subjective expression and the exploration of calligraphic effect. Court paintings enjoyed tremendous development, and enriched the nationwide painting boom, registering accomplishments that are not to be underestimated.

Continued a tradition established in the Later Tang and Later Han periods of the Five Dynasties, the Song Dynasty set up the Imperial Painting Academy to train painters for the court. At one time, emperor Huizong recruited painters through nationwide selections. Most emperors of the Song Dynasty showed varying degrees of interest in painting. emperor Huizong went to such an extreme that he was too preoccupied with painting and neglected the stately affairs as a consequence. At a time when his country

< *Singing and Dancing* (192.5cm×111cm), by Ma Yuan, collected by Beijing Palace Museum.

Listening to Guqin (147.2cm×52.3cm), by Zhao Jie, collected by Beijing Palace Museum.

was gravely endangered by domestic troubles and foreign aggressions, the emperor, a well established calligrapher and painter in his own right, scoured the nation not for talents to help save the country but for painting experts for the Imperial Painting Academy as well as famous paintings to add to his imperial collection. The Imperial Painting Academy became well established during the reigns of the emperor Huizong and emperor Gaozong, Zhao Gou (1127–1162). Under this general background to search for artistic talents many excellent folk painters established themselves and were recruited to the Imperial Painting Academy, which became a magnet to attract master painters. While maintaining some connections with society, court painters tended to go out of their way to please the monarch. They tried to maintain the traditional elegant style of the court art developed since the Tang Dynasty, and at the same time some of their works inevitably exhibited many typical Song Dynasty characteristics such as decadence, frail beauty and simplicity. emperor Huizong had a large collection of calligraphy and paintings, and so did his ministers and scholar-officials. *Xuanhe Collections of Paintings* recorded in details the court's rich art collections. When the Northern Song Dynasty fell in the Jingkang Incident, the Jin troops looted Bianjing. Some court painters were abducted to the north. The paintings in the court collection were taken out of the imperial palaces and scattered in the north. They had a major influence on the painting in Jin-controlled regions. Also, many painters traveled south as refugees and were employed in the emperor Gaozong's Imperial Painting Academy, enhanced the cultural development south of the Yangtze River. Famous court paintings of

Plucking Roses (27.2cm×90.5cm), by Li Tang, collected by Beijing Palace Museum.

the Song Dynasty include Guo Xi's *Early Spring* (*Zaochun Tu*) and *Spring Snow in Mountains* (*Guanshan Chunxue Tu*), Zhang Zeduan's *Along the River During the Qingming Festival* (*Qingming Shanghe Tu*), Wang Ximeng's *Thousands Li of Rivers and Mountains* (*Qianli Jiangshan Tu*), Li Tang's *Plucking Roses* (*Caiwei Tu*) and *Whispering Pines in the Mountains* (*Wanhe Songfeng Tu*), Ma Yuan's *Singing and Dancing* (*Tage Tu*) and *Waters* (*Shui Tu*).

Scholar painting, which first appeared in the Tang Dynasty, evolved to become a major artistic trend in the middle and late Northern Song Dynasty. At the time, there was a widespread interest in collecting and reviewing paintings among the scholar and scholar-officials. Quite a few of them took up painting as well. Like writing poems, they considered painting to be a way of expressing their unique self. Scholar painters had their own thoughts on the choice of subject and form. They trailed a new blazing in painting as they inscribed phrases and poems to decorate their paintings. In the Northern and Southern Song Dynasties, Chinese plum blossoms by Zhongren and Yang Wujiu, bamboos by Wen Tong, bizarre trees and stones by Su Shi, cloudy mountains by Mi Fu and his son Mi Youren and daffodils by Zhao Mengjian were particularly famous. One important contribution made by scholar-officials of the Northern Song Dynasty to scholar painting is their theoretical research. Ouyang Xiu proposed to pursue an aesthetic atmosphere of "desolateness and asceticism." Su Shi believed that it is childish to judge a painting by its formal resemblance, denying the notion that painting mainly aims at imitating nature. As a Chinese tradition, scholar-officials had long formed a network, through which scholar painting and the ideas of Su Shi and others spread rapidly, even to Liao and Jin territories ruled by ethnic minorities, becoming a precursor of the scholar painting of the Yuan and Ming dynasties.

Along the River During the Qingming Festival (Qingming Shanghe Tu)

Compared with the Tang Dynasty, figure paintings of the Five Dynasties and the Northern and Southern Song dynasties covered more subjects such as religious mythology, historical stories, and scholar life and so on. Most painters laid emphasis on the description of the figures' facial expressions and inner feelings with an enhanced ability to convey the mental states. Painting skills evolved in two directions: Meticulous style featured fine brushwork and rich colors, using more color tones than the Tang Dynasty; and in the ink-and-wash school, there emerged a freehand style with Liang Kai's works as a representative in addition to Li Gonglin and Zhang Zeduan, who were masters of outline drawing.

In the Tang and Song dynasties, Chinese painters tended to use tranquil colors, and simple and unsophisticated strokes. Following the steps of Gu Kaizhi and Wu Daozi, Li Gonglin (1049–1106), a painter in the North Song Dynasty, was famous for outline drawing characterized by "supple brushwork, diluted ink and absence of color and wash." Outline drawing is a technique originally used to draft a painting, like sketching in Western painting. After Wu Daozi, painting critics came to realize that a combination of painting and calligraphy would make single-colored drawings worthy of appreciation just like calligraphy. Outline drawing can produce a marvelous effect without the use of colors. *Taoist Gods*

Visiting the Primeval Lord of Heaven (*Chaoyuan Xianzhang Tu*) is the most famous painting of the outline drawing style in the Northern Song Dynasty. Preserved to this day thanks to the efforts of modern Chinese painting master Xu Beihong, it provides a strong testament to the mesmerizing charm of outline drawing. Li Gonglin also went down in the history of Chinese painting as a master of outline drawing with his unique paintings, such as *Five Horses* (*Wuma Tu*), *Illustrations of Jiuge* (*Jiuge Tu*), *Portrait of Vimalakirti* (*Weimojie Tu*) and *Imitating Wei Yan's Herding the Ranch* (*Lin Weiyan Fangmu Tu*), all of which are regarded as textbooks of outline drawing. Images depicted by simple brush strokes are not only perfectly vivid but also as rhythmic as calligraphy with distinctive appeal.

Gong Kai (c.a. 1222–1304), a painter of the outline drawing school in the Southern Song Dynasty, also learned from Wu Daozi, but adopted a more wild style. He liked painting ghosts and was particularly famous for his portrayal of Zhong Kui. His *Zhong Kui Traveling With His little Sister* (*Zhongshan Chuyou Tu*) depicts an excursion of Zhong Kui and his sister, who were each on a sedan carried by ghosts. Despite the evident gloominess, the painting was full of artistic glamour. Gong's paintings were usually rife with punchy satire. Critics in the Yuan Dynasty believed his paintings were not to be appreciated lightheartedly. Liang Kai (birth and death years unknown) in the Southern Song Dynasty, a painter once in the Imperial Painting Academy, was also skilled at painting human figures in the outline drawing style. However, according to historical records, he changed style in his middle age, from outline drawing to ink-and-wash freehand painting—a free, unconstrained style of painting comparable to wild cursive calligraphy and characterized by varying shades of ink. His enduring paintings in latter style include *The Six Patriarchs* (*Liuzu Tu*), *Immortal in Splashed Ink* (*Pomo Xianren Tu*) and *Li Bai Chanting Poems to the Moon* (*Taibai Xingying Tu*).

Zhang Zeduan's *Along the River During the Qingming Festival* was painted on silk with light colors. Most of the images were outlined

Along the River During the Qingming Festival (24.8cm×527.8cm), by Zhang Zeduan, collected by Beijing Palace Museum.

by black strokes, exemplifying the characteristics of painting of the Song Dynasty—neatness and fineness. A vivid reproduction of the prosperous Bianliang (today's Kaifeng), the 24.8-cm-high and 528-cm-long scroll is an unrivaled work of art of the 12th century. As a court painting, the *Qingming* scroll is unlike ordinary "folkloric paintings." Lively, humorous folkloric scenes can easily be found in *Itinerant Vendors* (*Huolang Tu*), *Children at Play* (*Xiying Tu*) and other paintings by mediocre painters such as Su Hanchen and Li Song. In the *Qingming* scroll, Zhang Zeduan gave a panoramic description of the activities of all walks of life on the Qingming Festival in Bianjing (present-day Kaifeng, He'nan province) from a bird's-eye view as soberly and objectively as possible, making the spectacular scroll a historical epic. The scroll features scholars, farmers, business people, doctors, fortune tellers, Buddhists, Taoists, petty officials, women, boat trackers, cattle, horses, camels, various shops along streets, rivers, ports, lakes, swamps, boats, official compounds, large mansions and thatched houses. Boasting a keen observation of life, an acute mind and an excellent mastery of painting composition, Zhang was well-rounded painter skilled at portraying human figures, mountains and rivers and various forms of architecture, as evidenced by the animated, lifelike facial expressions, deftly painted trees and ripples and the seamless transition from one scene to another in the *Qingming* scroll. Incorporating all sophisticated painting techniques in the Song Dynasty, the scroll looks complex yet orderly. In particular, the human figures are so skillfully portrayed that each of them can be closely examined. Zhang painted the scroll with a prudent attitude comparable to that of a historian. Using exaggeration and a comic atmosphere typical of folkloric paintings, he reproduced the social customs and lifestyles at the time, transportation on the crucial traffic artery Bianhe River and the hard life of the working people, busy scenes that reveal his meditative thoughts.

The *Qingming* scroll does not carry the painter's signature. In his postscript to the scroll, Zhang Zhu of the Jin Dynasty

Part of *Along the River During the Qingming Festival.*

ascribed it to Zhang Zeduan, a native of Dongwu (in present-day Shandong province), whose birth and death years were unknown. He pursued studies in Bianliang, the capital of the Northern Song Dynasty, and was admitted to the Imperial Painting Academy as a court painter. According to Zhang Zhu, he was good at "boundary painting," a type of landscape or figure painting with architecture as background and used to depict cities, streets and boats. Since its completion, the *Qingming* scroll has been widely recognized as a valuable painting. Many reproductions of the scroll were available in the Southern Song Dynasty. They were sold in the galleries in Lin'an at one gold coin per scroll, a fact that testified to the scroll's special popularity. Different from ordinary folkloric painting, court painting and scholar painting, the *Qingming* scroll is not only aesthetically impressive but also informative and revealing. It is truly a treasure among the world's ancient paintings.

Panorama *Shanshui*

By the Song Dynasty, landscape had risen to dominate the Chinese painting. Painters traveled extensively into forests and

Appreciation of Masterpieces
Chinese painting masterpieces are to be appreciated from three aspects: first, the paintings themselves, such as style, composition, brushing, and color; second, the calligraphic standard of the painters' signatures, including their positions, fonts, sizes, and the consistency between handwriting and painting style; and third, the style, size and school of the painters' seals, the match of characters cut in intaglio and relief, and the position of the seals, as well as the correctness of the texts and the consistency between the texts and the painting.

mountains where they spent days observing nature in an effort to accurately reproduce natural beauty in different places, seasons and kinds of weather in an impressive manner. Guo Xi, a landscape painter in the Northern Song Dynasty, wrote in his book on painting Spirituality by Forest Stream, "To capture the essence of nature requires a keen interest in painting, hard work and extensive traveling." From imposing mountains and rivers exquisitely portrayed, to miniature scenes briefly depicted, all landscapes represented eminent creations of different periods. Such paintings were not only of sublime mountains dotted with splendid architecture, aristocrats' excursions to luxurious gardens and scholar-officials' secluded life, but also of rural scenery across the country featuring the life of ordinary people such as driving a cart, running a watermill, ferrying, farming, fishing, wood logging and riding on a mule as well as places such as Buddhist and Taoist temples and wine shops in deserted cities. Painters classified shanshuis into various categories, each of which had distinctive characteristics. For example, the scenery "in the north" and that "south of the Yangtze River" differed greatly. Other formulized subjects included "morning mist," "evening green," "summer mountains," "cold forests," "remote valleys," "gentle breeze and light rain," "waters and skies blending into one color," "rivers rushing through a valleys," "evening sun in sparse forests," "slight snow in a fishing village," "desolate temples in autumn mountains," "buffalo boy returning home by a willow-lined river," and "fishing alone in winter." They also illustrated ancient poems through realistic depiction of actual landscape while using imagination.

XiaoXiang River (50cm×141cm), by Dong Yuan, collected by Beijing Palace Museum.

In the Song Dynasty, northern panorama shanshui, initiated by Jing Hao, a painter in the Five Dynasties, continued to enjoy wide popularity. Jing's vertical scrolls were symbolic to those longing for a secluded life in that they resemble towering mountains and screens that separate their long-coveted world of freedom with the real world beset with disturbances and disasters. Three painters of the Northern Song Dynasty, Li Cheng, Guo Xi and Fan Kuan, pushed this genre to its peak. Since the Six Dynasties, Chinese landscape painting had been influenced not only by Confucianism but also by Taoism and Buddhism, with the combination of Confucian rationalism and Taoist non-action as its fundamental feature. Either to become an official by taking the imperial civil service exam or to live a secluded life was the code of life of the scholars. For example, according to historical records, Li Cheng was a "knowledgeable and talented" man with "big ambitions since childhood." Of course, the phrase, "big ambitions," does not mean that he wanted to become a successful artist. Instead, it indicates Li's political ambitions. However, as he "failed one exam after another, getting nowhere in the end," Li decided to "devote himself to painting," "spending most of his days in mountain caves painting cold forests." Guo Xi also pointed out in Spirituality by Forest Stream that the reason why gentlemen enjoyed mountains and rivers was that these natural landscapes make them "feel closer to the hermits living as fishermen and wood loggers in isolation to the troublesome world."

Li Cheng (919–967) was almost a contemporary of Jing Hao and Guan Tong. A descendant of the royal clan of the Tang Dynasty, he lived in Chang'an but later moved to Yingqiu, Qingzhou (present-day Shandong province), gaining a nickname of Li Yingqiu. Li Cheng was good at writing poems, playing zither and playing chess, but he had never been an official in his lifetime. He first learned from Jing Hao and Guan Tong, and then developed his own style as he concentrated on depicting actual landscapes. Most of his paintings were of cold forests from a "level-distance perspective," or from near mountains across to distant mountains. They were distinguished by their brevity and sharpness and the use of diluted ink. Li was endowed with an amazing vision of nature. Although he began his painting career by learning from Jing and Guan, his early works were not too much influenced by stereotypes. *Level-Distance View of Pines* (*Qiaosong Pingyuan Tu*) features true-to-life scenery that we are used to admiring. It is a rarity among Chinese landscapes as it conforms to the laws of perspective, with the pine trees nearby appearing much higher than the remote mountains. We will not think the painter was mistaken in making the trees higher than the mountains. Li Cheng was so faithful to his own observations of nature that he adopted the level-distance perspective in most of his works, thereby giving the scenes a sense of broadness. Following Jing Hao in terms of brushwork, he focused on the "backbone" of the mountains and trees to create a feeling of desolateness, serenity and remoteness. What is remarkable about him is that he stressed realistic representation of nature in depicting forests and rocks while rejecting all stereotypes. *Reading the Tablet by a Jagged Rock* (*Dubei Keshi Tu*) is a perfect representation of a serene, bleak natural view. On the slope of a mountain grows an ancient tree, whose sparse twigs are twined by vines. There is nothing in the background as if the boundless place has been lying barren for a long time, a scene that leaves viewers in melancholy. A magnificent tablet is poised on

Reading the Tablet by a Jagged Rock (126.3cm×104.9cm),by Li Cheng,collected by Osaka Municipal Museum of Art.

a terrace. It sits on a tortoise-shaped pedestal with dragon carvings on its top. A man wearing a hat is reading the inscriptions on the tablet on the back of a mule. A boy, presumably the man's valet, stands beside him with a stick in his hand. The trees and the stones were outlined before they were painted with ink, looking clear and vigorous.

Li Cheng, Guan Tong and Fan Kuan represented three major

Level-Distance View of Rocks (120.8cm×167.7cm), by Guo Xi, collected by Beijing Palace Museum.

schools of landscapes in north China during the Five Dynasties and the Northern Song Dynasty. By the Northern Song Dynasty, Li Cheng's paintings had become rare. Mi Fu went as far as suggesting that genuine Li's paintings were nonexistent. *A Solitary Temple Amid Clearing Peaks* (*Qingluan Xiaosi Tu*) currently kept in the Nelson-Atkins Museum of Art in the United States is said to be a work of Li Cheng. Although most of Li Cheng's paintings have not survived today, it is still not difficult to sense his style from the paintings of his many followers. His most well known disciples include Wang Shen, Xu Daoning, and Guo Xi.

Guo Xi, art named Chunfu, was a native of Wenxian, Henan Province. He was admitted to the Imperial Painting Academy in his middle age and served as a court painter until his death. He was said to been a favorite courtier of emperor Shenzong of the Northern Song Dynasty. A disciple of Li Cheng and an outstanding landscape painter in his own right, his painting was characterized by vigorous brushwork and clear ink-and-wash style. He depicted mountains and rocks using light ink strokes like rolling clouds. The dangling twigs in his paintings resemble crab legs. He employed an exquisite style in his early years, but later he shifted to an imposing one. He was particularly good at reproducing towering precipice, pines, winding rivers, cliffs and sheer peaks shrouded in mist. He is often mentioned together with Li Cheng as "Li-Guo." Guo's representative works include *Early Spring* (*Zaochun Tu*) and *Spring Snow in Mountains* (*Guanshan Chunxue*), *Level-Distance View of Rocks* (*Keshi Pingyuan*) and *Silent Valley* (*Yougu*). In *Spirituality by Forest Stream*, a collection of his essays on painting complied by his son Guo Si, Guo Xi suggested that a landscape should give viewers a feeling as if they were present on the scene, where they can take a stroll, feast their eyes, have fun and take a brief retreat. He also encouraged the painters to travel extensively and observe everything closely in an effort to learn from nature. He also summarized the painters' observation skills into three perspectives —remoteness in height, remoteness in depth and remoteness in horizon.

Early Spring, collected in the TaipeiPalace Museum, is a breathtaking landscape. It is a vivid depiction of the early spring season when everything is teeming with life, featuring thin mists, new leaves and limpid rivers. The human figures, boats and buildings are all arranged according to the major theme of the picture. It has a distinctive layout and is quiet and spacious in artistic conception with bizarre rocks and striking mountains. As a student of Li Cheng, Guo Xi tried to keep his painting as close as possible to the deep wilderness while exhibiting the magnificent style of landscape in north China and the regular style typical of court painters. He used the three perspectives alternatively, with mountains far and near setting off one another amidst lingering, graceful mist. "The painting easily generates a sense of 'remoteness' —a space is nourishing to the heart of the viewers. However, judging from this painting, which highlights paths in mountains, boats on the rivers and pedestrians on the roads, the painter's

Early Spring (158.3cm×108.1cm), by Guo Xi, collected byTaipei Palace Museum.

proposal of giving viewers a feeling as if they were present on the scene, where they can view, walk, travel and live, is a nothing but an assumption, or an ideal that may not necessarily be put into practice." As a matter of fact, the structure of vertical scrolls constrains painters' attempts to convey the relative remoteness which they consider necessary to create an ideal composition of landscape. However, as they gained a good command of this form of painting, which reached maturity in their time, their observation of and experience with nature, deepened in an unprecedented manner. Guo Xi's *Early Spring* provides evidence to the contradiction.

More realistic and less grand paintings by Guo Xi have a different aesthetic conception. *Level-Distance View of Rocks* (1078 AD) only used the horizontal perspective. The relative relationship between the nearby pines and rocks to faraway mountains is reminiscent of Li Cheng's works. With this more simplistic perspective, the view is manipulated and adapted by the painter, thus leaving more room for expressing his personal feelings. This approach of composition allows the maximum exploitation of varying ink tones. The scenes nearby are outlined in firm strokes and painted by "curled cloud lines," while mountains in the distance are painted in light ink using the "boneless method." The dimly discernible landscape was reproduced as natural as possible. Guo's paintings of "corner view" laid the groundwork for the painting style of the Southern Song Dynasty.

Fan Kuan was a native of Huayuan (Yaoxian), Shaanxi Province. The dates of his birth and death are unkown. His mild temper earned him a nickname Fan Kuan (Kuan means mild tempered in Chinese). He lived in early Northern Song Dynasty and was one of the three most famous landscape painters of the Northern Song Dynasty. He first learned from Li Cheng and then from Jing Hao before he retreated to mountains in the belief that "Nature is a better teacher than people." He established his own style based on his observation of nature, becoming a representative

Travelers in Streams and Mountains (206.3cm×103.4cm), by Fan Kuan, collected byTaipei Palace Museum.

of the "north school" along with Li Cheng. Fan was a painter who would sit somewhere in remote mountains all day along, examining the landscapes all around and pondering over the "real nature". He was very good at depicting scenes of the four seasons, travelers, and unaccountable views of winds, the moon, clouds and skies after rain or snow. All his paintings are magnificent landscapes of Shaanxi and Gansu provinces. They were painted on broad scrolls with striking mountain views. He liked to draw lush forests on top of the mountains and protruding rocks in the middle of rivers using "raindrop strokes," which underscore the tangible structure and texture of the mountains. His famous works include *Travelers in Streams and Mountains* (*Xishan Xinglv Tu*) and *Snow in a Cold Forest* (*Hanlin Xuejing*).

Travelers in Streams and Mountains was painted on silk by ink. On the side of the painting are writings by Dong Qichang of the Ming Dynasty, "*Xishan Xinglv Tu* by Fan Zhongli of the Northern Song Dynasty." A representative work of Fan Kuan, the painting depicts a spectacular view of Qinglong Moutains, exuberant forests and grasses, imposing rocks and waving ridges. It seems that Fan paid no heed to the traditional painting layout that emphasized the depth of the scene. Instead, he put the steep precipice in the center, indicating the mountain's "existence" was of great importance to the hermit in the painting. For him, the mountain is what a philosopher would call "entity" and symbolizes the "spiritual enlightenment" that he pursues. The hermit sits in the mountains, completely integrating himself into the nature. Despite the use of "raindrop strokes," which can be interpreted as an appropriate way to express his feelings, Fan devoted great attention to impressive details. He portrayed rivers in the valley, broad riverbeds and roads at the foot of the mountain, donkeys carrying firewood and wayfarers hurrying on their journey in a regular, scrupulous manner, like dry-point works of European rural life in the 17th century.

In the Five Dynasties and the Northern Song Dynasty, Chinese landscape painters, from north China's Jing Hao, Li Cheng, Fan Kuan and Guo Xi to Dong Yuan in the south, established a complete set of patterns for Chinese landscape painting. Meanwhile, realistic representation of nature remained top concern of most painters. They were trying to find a perfect expression for the landscapes which they constantly attempted to improve with their direct observations and personal experiences of the nature, thereby establishing a model for landscape. The grand scale and composition of the works and the implicit philosophic meanings they expressed were unrivaled by later paintings. However, Shanshuis are fundamentally different from the Western landscapes, which aim to reproduce natural scenes in a physical sense through illusion and imitation. The nature reflected on silk or paper scrolls in ink is suggestive, totally different from the actual nature that we perceive. While the Chinese are accustomed to such suggestive landscapes, viewers who prefer Western painting traditions tend to interpret these refreshingly pleasant paintings to be landscapes of unique expressionists.

Su Shi and Mi Fu

As a great author, frustrated politician and amateur painter, Su Shi occupied a significant position in the history of Chinese painting despite only a few of his paintings have survived today. That is because Su, active during the Northern Song Dynasty, was not only the first person to propose the concept of "scholar painting," but also a founder and practitioner of this new style. After him, scholar painting gradually became the mainstream of

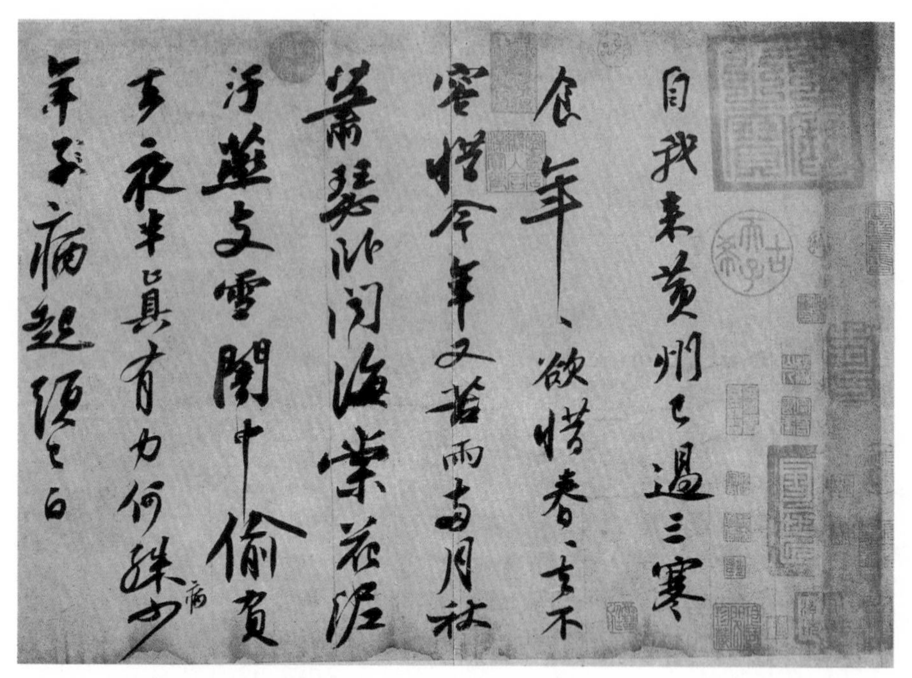

Handwriting on *Poem of Hanshi Festival in Huangzhou* (34.2cm×18.9cm), part, by Su Shi, collected byTaipei Palace Museum.

Chinese painting.

Su Shi (1037–1101), art named Zizhan and also known as Dongpo Jushi, was a native of Meishan, Sichuan Province. He entered the civil service as a youth and was promoted to a prominent position in the imperial court. However, as a middle-aged man, he was jailed for his involvement in a political incident and was exiled several times. He did not receive amnesty till the time when he was on the verge of death. Having experienced so many ups and downs in his life, Su had an extremely complex philosophical view, encompassing "the golden mean" and "the heavenly fate and destiny" of Confucian, the serenity and the contentment without disgrace of philosophic Taoism, the detachment and enlightenment of Buddhism and the metaphysical pursuit of longevity of religious Taoism. Not a professional painter, Su painted only occasionally, most of withered trees, bamboos and bizarre stones. Su's works survived today are all marked by the writings and poems of Mi Fu and Liu Zuoliang, which have ensured the identity of these paintings.

Poetry and painting were purely Su's hobbies. However, according to the Confucian standards of a "gentleman," Su strongly believed where art should belong—"artistic skill is the nearest equivalent to the truth." It means that in addition to physical and mental relaxation, scholars can gain a deeper understanding of the truth by studying fine arts. Su said natural images do not have an unchangeable normal state and therefore imperfections in certain aspects serve as evidence to their multifaceted nature, adding that violation of the common principles of truth will lead to a complete failure. The following is his comment on a painting of his friend Wen Tong (1018–1079):

When Wen Tong paints bamboos, all he sees is bamboos. As he integrates himself into the bamboos, his paintings look endlessly fresh.

Wen Tong was adept at painting bamboos. Unlike laypeople and craft painters who tend to focus on every detail, he concentrated only on bamboos so that he could integrate himself into nature and achieve a harmony in which the scenes he depicted would carry his feelings towards the nature, a style that Su Shi highly appreciated. When they enjoy natural landscapes, scholars will immediately go beyond the physical existence to reach a spiritual dimension, getting entertained and relaxed from this experience. Su sneered at painters who mechanically pursued the likeliness to nature. "Despite his superb expertise, Wu Daozi is merely a craft painter," he commented bluntly. The painters who Su admired most were not the omnipotent painters like Wu Daozi, but those well educated scholar painters who were capable of "going beyond the images" such as Wang Wei and Wen Tong. These painters could transcend formal likeliness to arrive at "common principles," using natural images as a means to express their inner feelings. They naturally combined images with human will, thereby expressing their unique self with their painting brushes.

A *Lucky Pine in Spring Mountain* (62.5cm×44cm), by Mi Fu, collected byTaipei Palace Museum.

A gentleman can put his thoughts into an object, but should not be obsessed with it. If he puts his thoughts into it, he will take pleasure from an insignificant object, while not being burdened by a valuable one. If he is obsessed with it, he will be burdened by an insignificant object, while taking no pleasure from a valuable one.

What matters to scholar painters is how to express the nature in their mind through images. They should transcend the images instead of being confined to them. If they give too much attention on images, they will become subordinated to them, only to find themselves frustrated in their pursuit of happiness. However, if they can go beyond the images, they can take pleasure from them, no matter how insignificant they are. Su's values were a negation to the criteria of the Northern Song Dynasty for the refined paintings. He further distinguished scholar painters from craft or career painters. It is his belief that the scholar painters are concentrated on "the spirit," while the latter only touch on the "surface." Seeking

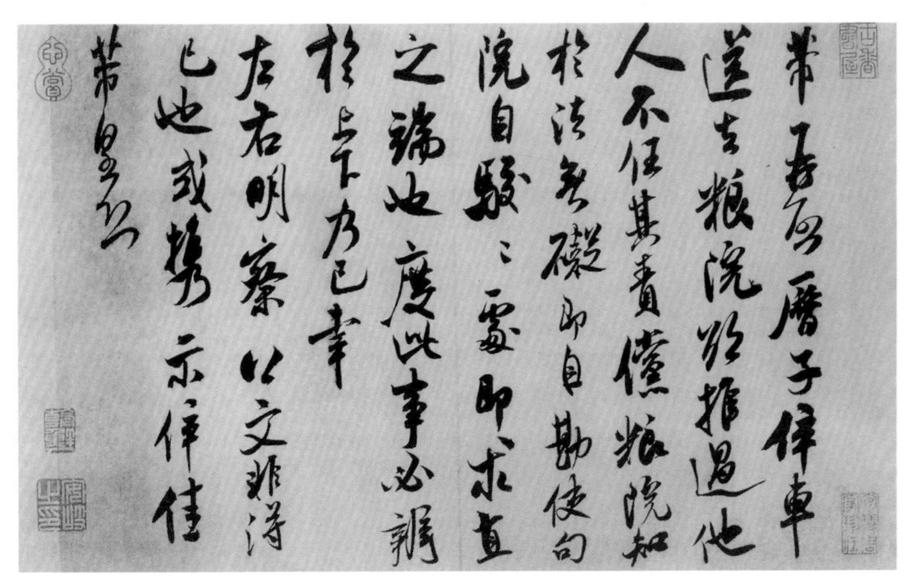

Handwriting on *Tiaoxi Brook Poems* scroll (189.5cm×30.3cm), part, by Mi fu, collected by Beijing Palace Museum.

likeliness to nature is the goal of craft painters, which scholars should not bother. Scholar painters should instead concentrate on improving morality and nurturing spirituality. In Su's opinion, the reason why likeliness should not be valued is that its pursuit will result in a further deviation from "the truth." What scholar painters seek to express is the "common principles" embodied in their characters and aspirations that only outstanding talents can understand. As a person with remarkable accomplishments in literature and distinctive personal charisma, Su was qualified enough to put forward this view, but whether his paintings can illustrate his theory is slightly a different matter. For Confucian scholars, poetry, calligraphy and painting are all forms of art which they enjoy as a mean of relaxation. Su said, "What cannot be fully expressed by poetry can be expressed by calligraphy or painting, both of which are ink creations." His casually painted *Bamboos and Stones* (*Zhushi Tu*) may be deemed as an example of scholar painters' improvised calligraphic painting. It is reminiscent of

Liang Kai's freehand-style paintings of poets and celestials in the Southern Song Dynasty. However, despite the prevailing painting style of the court and the Imperial Painting Academy at the time, the theories and works of eminent intellectuals such as Su Shi and Mi Fu clearly indicated a shift of painters' focus.

Mi Fu (1051–1107), a friend of Su's, was good at poems, essays, calligraphy and painting. He was also an expert of verifying the authenticity of paintings and a collector of famous works. Mi and Su were both maters of calligraphy. They were known as "Four Great Calligraphers" of the Song Dynasty together with Cang Xiang and Huang Tingjian. Art named Dong Yuan, Mi exhibited an innocently irregular style in his landscapes, most of which were in ink. Mi Youren (1086–1165), Mi Fu's son, or "junior Mi" as he is normally called, carried on the family tradition and was particularly adept at painting cloudy mountains. He made a slight change to his father's style, giving birth to a new school of landscape. Terms such as "Mi's mountains," "Mi's cloudy mountains" and "the Mi school" are often used in the study of Chinese painting history. Mi's mountains usually consist of brief strokes and are enveloped in changing clouds. Mi Fu said, "I paint in a casual manner. Most of my paintings feature trees and rocks hidden behind clouds and mists and are not literal representation of nature." In a similar fashion, junior Mi often humorously called his paintings "games with ink" in the postscripts.

In terms of artistic conception, Su Shi stood for "remoteness, freshness, brevity, and detachedness" while Mi Fu advocated "naturalness," "innocence" and "classical taste." Their viewpoints coincide, but Mi, being aggressive in nature, was more outspoken. Widely recognized masters of the landscape of the Tang and Song Dynasties were mostly from northern China such as Wu Daozi, Li Cheng and Guan Tong. Mi Fu, however, said that his paintings "are not as vulgar as those of Li Cheng and Guan Tong" and "have definitely no similarity to Wu Daozi's style." He also showed disapproval to court painters such as Guo Xi. However, he was ready to sing praise for Su Shi, who hardly stood out as a famed painter, for his occasional paintings of trees, bamboos and rocks. He was particularly fond of Dong Yuan, a neglected painter in southern China, repeatedly lauding him with his most positive comments. The reason seemed to be that Mi Fu found a similarity between Dong's paintings and the paintings 100 years before. His comments also served as an artistic manifesto of the scholar landscape painters with him as a representative:

People of the Suburb of Longsu (156cm×160cm), by Dong Yuan, collected by Taipei Palace Museum.

Dong Yuan, with his natural and innocent style, is unrivaled in the Tang Dynasty and is even better than Bi Hong. His works have no match in recent years for their profound spiritual dimension. Featuring rolling mountains and changing clouds and mists, his unembellished paintings convey a sense of innocence. Dark green mists and sturdy twigs are also vividly depicted. With streams, rivers, bridges, isles and fishermen, the paintings represent typical scenery of southern China.

The notion of "painting cloudy mountains as a game with ink" proposed by Mi Fu and his son Mi Youren is an indication of the scholar painters' style. Mi Fu's comments on Dong Yuan can generally be used to characterize his own paintings as well. Some critics point out while Dong tried to capture the structural changes of actual mountains and trees, the Mi's only played with ink casually, making almost no effort in that regard. That is because they were strongly influenced by Su Shi's uninhibited style of painting. Mi Youren's *Clearing Clouds Over Distant Peaks* (*Yuanxiu Qingyun Tu*), the remote mountains are not even outlined. Instead, they were shaped with different shades of ink. Based not on reality but on a transient scene in the mind, the ink-and-wash painting embodies an unaccountably mysterious taste, or the alleged "real interest" of nature. It is strange to note that Mi Youren used lines typical of Gu Kaizhi and Zhan Ziqian to depict the clouds and mists in this painting, a fact that shows scholar painters like him not only tried to convey the "real interest" directly but also attempted to reenact some classical painting stereotypes.

Scholar Paintings

Birds' luster and the color in Autumn scroll (28.4cm×93.2cm), by Zhao Mengfu, collected by Taipei Palace Museum.

Zhao Mengfu and "Four Masters of the Yuan Dynasty"

The theory of scholar painting of the Northern Song Dynasty did not have great influence on painting in the Southern Song Dynasty. Under great pressures from the Kingdom of Jin in the north, the Southern Song Dynasty was on the edge of being conquered. Intellectuals of Han ethnic group who believed in Confucius went around, canvassing supports for resisting aggressors of foreign ethnic groups. They put their patriotic passion and anger towards foreign aggressors into their poetries and statements. However, the mild painting style sought for after the Tang and Song Dynasties was not suitable to express the strong and melancholy feelings and emotions. Imperial Art Academy of the Southern Song Dynasty might only have some second-class painters and they could only express their anger through unrestrained and incisive brushwork. To those Confucius scholars who were well educated, these works of second class artists were not qualified. In the Yuan Dynasty, the society established some normality after wars and scholar painters started to question and acted violently against the narrow painting style of the Southern Song Dynasty. Zhao Mengfu was their representative.

Genghis Khan united Mongolia in 13th century and rose rapidly. In 1271, Kublai Khan established the Yuan Empire in Dadu (Beijing) and conquered the Southern Song Dynasty in less than 12 years, thus assumed authority over the whole China. During the early stage of the Yuan Dynasty, in order to consolidate its rule, Kublai Khan learnt the art of government from the Confucius works and was courteous to Confucius officials. His successors continued to value Confucius and respect Taoism and established Kui Zhang Ge. Painting collector Ke Jiusi (1290–1343) was appointed to be Court Academician of Book Appreciation to check and classify all the books in the imperial collections. Zhao Mengfu (1254–1322), art named Zi'ang, was also known by his literary name Songxue Daoren, and was descendant of the royal family of the Song Dynasty. After the fell of the Song, Zhao Mengfu was recommended to the imperial court and was appointed a court official since the new empire was particularly interested in the descendants of the previous dynasty. He only resigned after Kublai Khan died. Zhao Mengfu followed Dong Yuan and Li Cheng in painting mountains and waters and followed Li Gonglin and Tang Ren in painting portraits and horses. His ink-bamboo and flower-and-bird paintings were famous for his painting style

Horse Drinking Water in the Suburb in Autumn scroll (23.6cm×59cm), by Zhao Mengfu, collected by Beijing Palace Museum.

Fishermen on Dongting Lake scroll (146.6cm×58.6cm), by Wu Zheng, collected byTaipei Palace Museum.

using the round and vigorous brushwork. He painted stones in hollow strokes and painted bamboos in calligraphic style. Dong Qichang of the Ming Dynasty commented: "His paintings had the style of painters of the Tang Dynasty but not that slender, and were as vigorous as paintings of the Northern Song Dynasty, but not that boorish." He could write gentle poems and make seals. His paintings include *Birds' Luster and the Color in Autumn* (*Quehua Qiuse Tu*), *Painting of Red-Clothed Arhats* (*Hongyi Luohan Tu*), *Youyu Qiuhe Tu*, *Horse Drinking Water in the Suburb in Autumn* (*Qiujiao Yinma Tu*) and *Happiness of Fishermen at the Riverside* (*Jiangcun Yule Tu*). He also wrote 10 volumes of *Songxue Zhai Wenji* (*Collective Works of Songxue Daoren*).

Zhao Mengfu insisted to reform the painting style of the Imperial Art Academy of the Southern Song Dynasty and considered that paintings should have a sense of tradition; otherwise, they were valueless even they were carefully painted. China had the tradition of changing in accordance with ancient systems. The Yuan Dynasty abandoned the imperial art academy established in the Southern Song Dynasty and Zhao Mengfu, a scholar painter who directly served the imperial court, had rather special status. Zhao Mengfu's proposal, to abandon the tradition established in the Southern Song Dynasty and go back to the culture roots of the previous dynasties, pleasured the rulers of the Yuan Dynasty. Consequently he hoped to create a new painting style by continuing the traditions of the Jin Dynasty, Tang Dynasty, Five Dynasties and Northern Song Dynasty. His proposal and his persuasive paintings led to the development of a trend of "going back to the ancients" among painters in the Yuan Dynasty.

Zhao Mengfu had two distinctive painting styles. One was fine brushwork with heavy colors and the other, bold and unconstrained brushwork of ink and wash. The former painting style illustrated his respects for the paintings of the Jin, Tang and Northern Song Dynasties. In his early age, he learnt from the paintings of the Jin and Tang Dynasties and the color of green was the most frequently

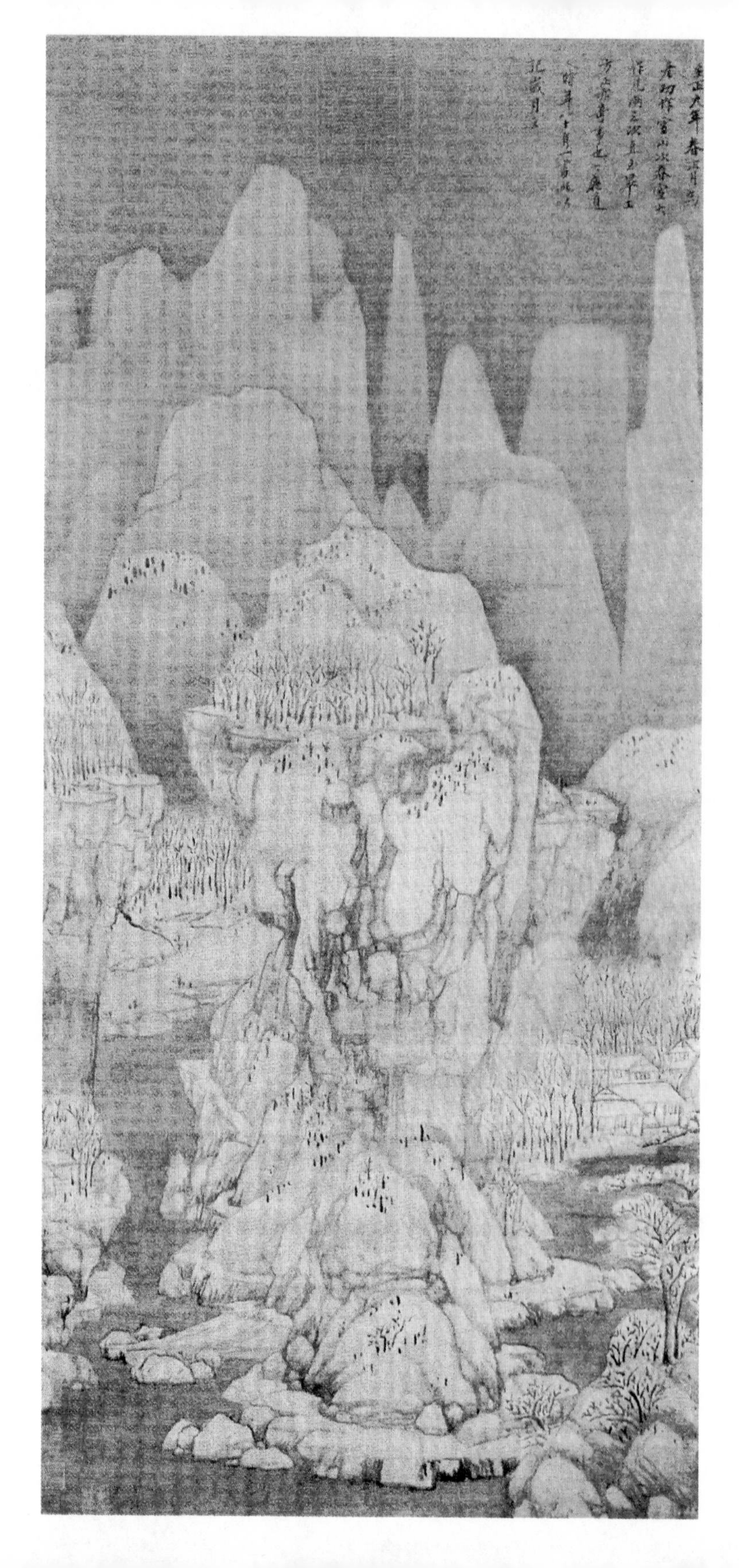

used. His painting of *Youyu Qiuhe Tu* was a good example. He drew sketch lines first and added color afterwards without texturing dots, which was a traditional style. *Horse Drinking Water in the Suburb in Autumn and Washing Horses* (*Yuma Tu*) followed the painting style of Tang Dynasty with carefully designed pattern and utilization of colors. The tone was warm and magnificent. Birds' luster and the color in Autumn embodied anther style with remote and simple landscape, which, according to Dong Qichang, followed the painting style of Dong Yuan. Modern art historian Wang Bomin (1924–present) made an on-the-spot investigation to Huabuzhu Mountain and Queshan Mountain that were painted in the painting, and confirmed that Zhao was a painting master who were good at painting real scenery. Ink painting *Water Village* (*Shuicun Tu*) exhibited the beautiful scene of range upon range of mountains covered with clouds and villages circled by rivers. He resumed the painting skill of using the centre of the brush and abandoned the Southern Song painters' practices of using sides of the brush. His ink landscapes seemed to be responding to Mi Fu's painting style. He also followed Li Cheng and Guo Xi, enabling him to rectify the shortcoming of hollowness evident in the Mi Fu's method. In order to express his respect for Su Shi and Wen Tong, he also imitated their styles and painted several bamboo and stone paintings, using his cool brushwork to remedy the curtness of Su Shi's painting. He consciously used calligraphic skill in his paintings and added large length of poetries. Experts say that scholar painting "started since Su Shi, and the gate widely opened since Zhao Mengfu."

Most of non-official scholar painters of the Yuan Dynasty had a tendency to retire from the secular world and to exercise painting freely in their spiritual world. They illustrated their way of living, and their interests and ambitions through paintings. Thus, mountains and waters, withered trees, bamboos and stones, plum blossoms and orchids became their favorite compositions while painting of figures that direct reflected social life had lost their favor. When considering paintings, scholar officials would

< *Nine Peaks after the Snow* (117.2cm×57.5cm), by Huang Gongwang, collected by Beijingi Palace Museum.

stress on the spirit of scholar, the sense of history, and the grace of non-convention and would object the sense of manipulation, or the sense of artisanship. Ink paintings of free-hand brush-works of Su Shi and Mi Fu were regarded as the best format to demonstrate this painting philosophy of scholars. Painters would pay great attentions to using calligraphic skills while painting and integrating poem and calligraphy into paintings. The use of calligraphy in paintings was used as criteria to judge their success. Scholar painters believed that people who were good at paintings must first be good at calligraphy and painting was just the extension of calligraphy skills. Scholar painters in the Yuan Dynasty pursued the painting theories of Wen Tong, Su Shi and Mi Fu of the Northern Song Dynasty, advocated abandoning actual appearance and seeking spiritual resemblance, and adopted the grace of simplicity. Though scholar paintings were regarded as art treasures, scholars still asserted that painting was only their spare time activities. Famous landscape painter Wu Zhen reiterated that "painting was simply an activity of interest while scholars were composing poems." Zhao Mengfu and Huang Gongwang, Wang Meng and Wu Zhen who rose in the middle and late Yuan Dynasty were regarded as "Four Masters of the Yuan Dynasty." In Late Ming Dynasty, Dong Qichang listed Zhao Mengfu separately as the grand master of the Yuan period, and added Ni Zan to the original "Four Masters of the Yuan Dynasty." These four people inherited the landscape tradition of the Five Dynasties and Northern Song Dynasty. They were influenced directly and indirectly by Zhao Mengfu but they had developed their own characteristics.

Huang Gongwang (1269–1354) was listed on the top of "Four Masters of the Yuan Dynasty." He was a child prodigy of many classical and historical works and showed talents on calligraphy, music and non-dramatic songs. However he learnt to paint rather late. He served as a local official in the Yuan Dynasty and was prosecuted by mistake in his middle age. After he was released, he lost faith in the administration and sought a live in seclusion.

He began to paint when he was 50 years old. Huang Gongwang further developed Zhao Mengfu's ink painting skill and exceeded the achievements of Dong Yuan and Juran. He used to texturing stroke. In his later years, he changed his painting style and rarely used the texturing stroke. The charms of his paintings were beyond those of Zhao Mengfu. His famous works survived include *Living in Fuchun Mountain* (*Fuchunshan Jutu*), *Cliff of Tianchi* (*Tianchi Shibi Tu*) and *Nine Peaks after the Snow* (*Jiufeng Xueji Tu*).

Wang Meng (1301–1385), art name Shuming, was also known by his literary name Xiangguang Jushi, or Huangheshan Qiao. He was Zhao Mengfu's nephew. He was born to a family of calligraphic and painting traditions. He served as an official but later resigned and chose to live in Huangheshan Mountain in Linping (now Yuhang of Zhejiang Province). After the fall of the Yuan Dynasty, he worked again as an official in Tai'an, Shandong Province. In 1385, he was arrested in association with the Huweiyong case and died in prison. He had a remarkable memory and read extensively with solid training in poetry, writing, calligraphy and painting. His paintings were influenced by Zhao Mengfu and often he received advices from Huang Gongwang. He also modeled Dong Yuan and Juran's style. He mainly paint ink paintings and developed the cow-hair strokes. He was regarded as a creative landscape master and almost all the painters of Ming and Qing Dynasties and modern painters learned from his paintings. His paintings survived include *Living in Summer Mountains* (*Xiari Shanju Tu*), *Living in Seclusion in Summer* (*Xiari Gaoyin Tu*) and *Gezhichuan Yiju Tu* (*Move to Live in Gezhi Valley*).

Ink painting Living in Summer Mountains was painted on paper, and is 118.1 cm high and 36.2 cm wide. It is now in the possession of Beijing Palace Museum. The remote part of the painting is ranges of mountains; the central part is a magnificent high mountain peak, thrusting into the cloud; the near part is ancient pine trees along hillside. Beside the trees is a pool of calm water and above the trees were rocks. On the rocks, was a bun-

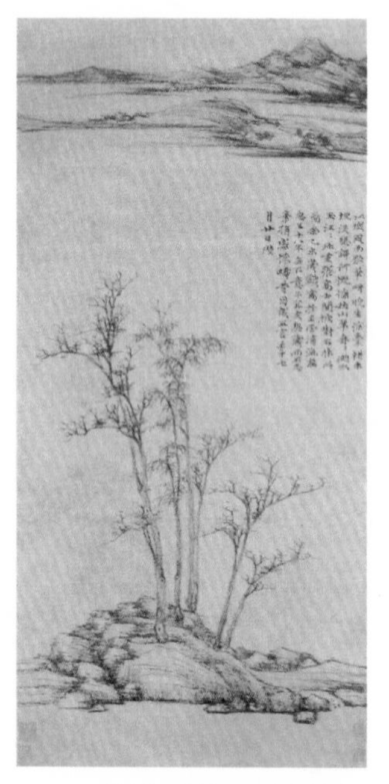

Fishing Village after Rains (96cm× 47cm), by Ni Zan, collected by Shang Hai Museum.

shape hill with its foot extended into water. Hills are divided into three layers with small pieces of sand lands dotting the spaces in between, mixing vague images with clear focuses. Ancient trees and treacherous mountains match well with brooks and water fall. the whole image is carefully arranged with totally different style to the paintings of the Yuan Dynasty. Judged from the postscript, the painting was completed in his later years.

Wu Zhen (1280–1354), art name Zhonggui, was also known Meihua Daoren, Meihua Shami or Meihua Heshang. He was born in Jiaxing of Zhejiang Province. He lived a seclusive life during his middle age and in poverty. He made a living by divination. Consequently he was called as "master of Taoist" and a "monk of Buddhist", which was not a rare phenomenon under the social background at that time. Wu Zhen modeled on Dong Yuan and Juran in painting landscape, trees and stones. Occasionally modeled on Jing Hao and Guan Tong. Yun Nantian, a landscape painter in the Ming Dynasty commented Wu's paintings, "Meihua Anzhu (Wu Zhen) and Yifeng Laoren (Huang Gongwang) learnt Dong Yuan and Juran's painting style together. Wu promoted obscurity while Huang adhere to simplicity. They had different aesthetics but similar artistic achievements." His paintings were most themed with fishermen, reflecting his life in seclusion and aloof social attitudes.

Ni Zan (about 1306–1374), was also known as Yunlinzi, Huanxiazi, Jingmanmin and Jingchu Yinzhe. He was born in Wuxi in a wealthy family. He built Qingbi Pagoda in his own garden and stored all his collections in the building. In his old age, he was longing for a reclusive living and sold all his lands and real estates. At that time, the society was in chaos, and he left home and lived on boats for 12 years. It was during that period when he devoted himself to painting and formed his own style in landscape. He was arrested because of his rebellion against taxation officials and died soon after his release. He was influenced greatly by Dong Yuan and also followed the styles of Jing Hao and Guan Tong. He also learnt from Li Cheng in painting mountains, stones and trees. His main compositions were the scenery around Tai Lake. Most of his paintings were constructed following a pattern where the lower section is flat hillside with bamboos and trees and huts or pavilions; the middle section is calm water and the top or the far section is ranges of mountains. He often used dry brushes with simply ink. His painting style of complexity and richness through simplicity exerted great influences to scholar painters of the Ming and Qing dynasties. His paintings survived include *Poem of Du Lin* (*Dulin Shiyi Tu*), *Shizilin Garden* (*Shizilin Tu*), *Fishing Village after Rains* (*Yuzhuang Qiuji Tu*) and *Six Men of Honor* (*Liu Junzi Tu*).

The ink-and-wash landscapes of "Four Masters of the Yuan Dynasty" marked the completion of change of interests in the landscapes formed in the Northern Song Dynasty. Dong Qichang summarized, "the four masters, Huang, Ni, Wu and Wang all started from learning from Dong Yuan and Juran," namely, the four masters established their own painting style enlightened by Dong Yuan. They established a future direction of landscapes for those followed. Later painters showed great respects for them, among whom the great painter, Shi Tao of the Qing Dynasty, famous for his egotism, commented, "the achievements of Dachi (Huang Gongwang), Yunlin (Ni Zan) and Huanghe Shanqiao (Wang Meng) exceeded those of the painters before them." Followers respected them not only because of their achievements made in the field of painting, but also their virtues and personalities. Huang Gongwang, Ni Zan, Wu Zhen and Wang Meng had very different personnel circumstances and experiences in their early years, but they reached the same goal in the end. They appreciated each other and shared a similar philosophic way of thinking. The four masters sought a life aloof from the secular society and tried to avoid the restrain of political ambitions and material temptations. They were men of principles and justice, and appreciated the seclusive life away from the normality of ordinary world. They were devout Taoist and Buddhist. They dreamt of living with the nature and making friends while wondering in mountains and rivers. Their highest gratification was lying in deep forests and by rivers and rocks, watching white clouds going by. The landscape was their religion.

Plum Blossom, Orchid, Bamboo and Stone

From the late Song Dynasty to the Yuan Dynasty, the days were gone when scholars and artists were imperially favored at the court. However realizing the importance of Confucius and Taoism in the society, the rulers had to install a few representatives and reluctantly looked for people such as Zhao Mengfu. Under this general background, most poets, artists and scholars chose to leave Hangzhou for other cities such as Suzhou and Yangzhou. "Four Masters of the Yuan Dynasty" all left that troubled capital. But Wang Meng and Ni Zan could still not escape and were implicated in court scandals, died unnaturally. The political and literature prosecution, and the corruption of mandarin class alienated the intellectual elites further away from the imperial court. They sought more often self gratification in pursuing the art of paintings without any political implications. As special items, the plum blossom, orchid, bamboo and stone (chrysanthemum) were used as favorite painting topics, and implicitly explored the common accepted characteristics associated with these plants. Orchid and bamboo represented moral loftiness and plum blossom and stone represented characteristics of principles and justice. Traditionally

Green Orchid for Hai Yan (33cm×126cm) , by Pan Tianshou, collected by Pan Tianshou Museum

they have been humanized and bamboo is called "gentleman" and orchid "beauty". Su Shi often painted bamboos, withered trees and strange stones in a very leisurely style. However, philosopher Zhu Xi of the Song period commented, "Su's paintings appear to be unintentional and very leisurely but a close examination will tell their proud and aloof characteristics which are a reflection of Su's own personality."

Similar to the fashion of landscapes in the period before, plum blossom, orchid, bamboo and stone (chrysanthemum) attracted the following of a new generation of painters which marked a historical change in the painting trends. During the Tang and Song Dynasties, both flower-and-bird and landscape became independent genres of Chinese paintings with a variety range of subjects. Some art historians even consider flower-and-bird paintings are earlier than those of landscape and began with the paintings of plants and animals on the potteries of the Neolithic Age. There were more than 80 artists listed on the official records in the Tang Dynasty who were the specialists on painting flowers, trees, birds and animals, and many of them painted flowers or birds only. Flower-and-bird paintings once were the major compositions attracting the interest of the imperial court. Of the Five Dynasties (907–960 AD) the imperial painter Huang Quan's (903–965 AD) works featuring delicate brushwork and heavy color was the representative of its kind. The painter lived in the imperial court for most of his life and was famous for his paintings of rare birds, animals, flowers and stones in the royal collections. Xu Xi, another important painter of the same period, on the contrary considered his imperial topic and style extravagant and wasteful and would rather explore the topic of ordinary rivers and forests and sought paintings of outside world. He was famous for light color and ink paintings of flowers, birds, fish, insects, and fruits and vegetables. However, both the rich imperial style of Huang Quan, and the leisurely and wild style of Xu Xi were attaching great importance to sketch coping of real objects. Few authentic paintings of their paintings have survived. But During the heydays of the imperial art academy in the Song Dynasty and the Ming Dynasty, Huang Quan's Huang style was followed and promoted by the imperial artists while Xu Xi's style was copied and developed among the folk painters. A close examination of these flower-and-bird paintings, one would feel a similar sense as to study the landscapes of the Five Dynasties and Northern Song Dynasty, a sense of "natural theology." In this regard, *Xuanhe Collection of Paintings-Flowers and Birds* commented:

Peony among all kinds of flowers and phoenix and peacock among all kinds of birds represent rich and honor while pine tree, bamboo, plum blossom, chrysanthemum, gull, egret, wild goose and wild duck all represent free and leisure. The honorable dignity of cranes, the brave struggle of haws, the exquisite grace of aspen, willow and phoenix trees, and the forever morality of pine and cypress all can be vividly expressed in paintings. A person who appreciates the intention of painters would ponder and marvel the implicit of their shapes and lines and the spiritual fancy of the images in their minds. They could often gain much by studying the paintings as with the experience of real world.

Meticulous flower-and-bird painting style continued to develop, especially in the imperial court. Painters still devoted themselves to vividly portray flowers, grass, birds and animals. Plum blossom, bamboo, stone, orchid and grape became an independent painting genre and the fashion of scholar painting. According to *Xuanhe Collection of Paintings*, "Some paintings with light ink do not seek actual likeness, but the spiritual resemblance. These paintings are usually not painted by craft or career painters, but by scholars." These scholar painters included Su Shi and Wen Tong. They did not want to copy and paint meticulously the natural objects as their craft or career counterparts, and disregarded the imperial style of the court. They chose to paint objects such as strange stones and withered trees to reflect their spiritual thinking. Such paintings provided an ideal medium for them to express through their works. Compared with landscapes, flower-and-bird paintings could enable them to play the game of inks better, and could provide a painting format for them to combine poetry calligraphy, painting and seal engraving art into one piece, fully exhibiting authors' capabilities of the scholarship. There were also another kind of painters whose status was between the imperial craft painters and the scholars. They appreciated scholar painters' elegance, but indulged in the funs of meticulous paintings. There were many meticulous paintings in the Yuan Dynasty and the Ming Dynasty that were delicately painted only with ink. Flower-and-bird paintings of Wang Yuan (dates unknown) and Bian Wenjin (dates unknown) of the Ming Dynasty, Lin Liang (1426–1495) of the Yuan Dynasty and Shen Zhou, Wen Zhengming and Tang Yin of "Wu School" in the Ming period all belonged to this category.

Peony and Rocks (12.0.6cm×58.4cm), by Xu Wei.

Freehand brushwork of ink paintings with themes of plum blossom, bamboo, flower and bird in the Yuan Dynasty made an outstanding achievement. To those scholar officials who had to try to keep far from the reality of political affairs, Xu Xi's wildness-and-leisure style paintings of flower and bird could bring

Ink Grapes (116.4cm×64.3cm), by Xu Wei, collected by Beijing Palace Museum.

comforts to their hearts. Zhao Mengfu of the early Yuan Dynasty and three of the Four Masters of Yuan, Wang Meng, Ni Zan and Wu Zhen were all famous for painting bamboo and stone. Imperial scholar painter Ke Jiusi used ink paintings of bamboo to judge whether a painting was a piece of scholars." Wang Mian (1287–1359), born into a simple farmer family, chose to live a seclusive life in his hometown after failing the imperial examinations, calling himself Meihua Wuzhu (Master of Plum Blossom House). His ink paintings of plum blossom with refreshingly lucid style were of great natural charm. Xu Wei (1521–1593), a poet, painter and dramatis in the Mid Ming Dynasty, was regarded as the person who completed the transformation of flower-and-bird paintings from the classical style to the scholar style with inspirational significance to "greater freehand ink paintings" of the generations thereafter.

Xu Wei, art name Wenchang, also called Tianchi and Qingteng, was born in Shanyin (now Shaoxing), Zhejiang Province. His poetic drama Si Sheng Yuan in his early age was appreciated by the great dramatist of the Ming Dynasty, Tang Xianzu. Xu was in poverty all his life and failed imperial examinations several times, which once brought him the disaster of mental disorder. He killed his wife and was arrested. In his declining years, he was released from the jail, and died at the age of 73. His actual painting life only lasted for 10 years. He wrote a poem to describe himself:

Wandering aimlessly for half a life, I am getting old;

Standing alone at my study in night wind, I make a whistle in bold;

Looking at the bright pearls under the pen, nowhere to be sold;
Throwing it up and down among wild canes idly, I walk in cold.

Xu's flower-and-bird paintings and calligraphy was known as the "green vane style." It incorporated the elements of the Song and Yuan Dynasties and those of Shen Zhou and Lin Liang. In contrast against the idleness and grace of the "Wu School". it directly expressed his surging feelings. He boldly broke the limit of the shapes and injected the subjects with powerful personal feelings. He made use of the subjects under discussion to express his own emotions. Taking full advantages of Chinese painting paper (xuan paper), he wrote and painted freely to his heart to depict his subjects of spiritual likeness with moist and flowing ink. His existing masterpieces include *Peony and Rocks* (*Mudan Jiaoshi Tu*), *Putao Tu* (*Grapes*), *Ink Flowers* (*Mo Hua Tu*) and many others. Painter Zheng Xie of the Qing Dynasty, who was also one of the "Yangzhou Eight Eccentrics," highly appreciated the paintings of Xu Wei and said, "I would like to offer 50 gold for a branch of megranate of Tianchi (Xu Wei)." He engraved a seal, reading "Running Dog at the Door of the Green Cane" to express his admiration of Xu. Qi Baishi of the modern times also expressed his respect for Xu by saying he wished to be born 300 years ago to "tidy papers and grind ink blocks for the Green Cane."

Xu's painting style had great influence and inspiration significance to many painters of the Qing Dynasty, such as Zhu Da, Shi Tao and the "Yangzhou Eight Eccentrics," and the painters of modern times such as Wu Changshuo and Qi Baishi.

"The Southern and Northern Sects"

Zhao Mengfu of the early Yuan Dynasty raised the idea of "ancient sense," aiming at resuming the interest which was lost at the end of the South Song Dynasty and initiated a new style through the way of seeking classics of the previous generations. Zhao himself and "Four Masters of Yuan Dynasty" completed the

Picture Album of Mountains-and-Waters Paintings, part, by Shen Zhoui.

change of painting styles as they had expected. Then, after the fall of the Yuan, during the Ming and Qing dynasties, however the negative influences of the doctrine "back to the ancients" became evident and the practice of copying the ancient paintings prevailed in the world of painting. Even those trivial painters would label themselves as the admirers of Huang Gongwang. Painters in the Ming Dynasty had abandoned completely their researches for the nature. They still treasured the nature but only the nature in the ancient paintings. They were so keen to illustrate how their painting styles and brushworks or mountains and stones or trees on their paintings can be traced back to certain painters in the previous dynasties. They were so fond of the ancient paintings that they believed copying the paintings were the best way to achieve the pleasure of painting. Meanwhile, the commercial prosperity and colorful life in the South reduced the opportunity of going back to the nature and for the painters they considered it was unnecessary to do so at all.

The Ming Dynasty resumed the imperial art academy which was abandoned during the Yuan Dynasty and the centre of scholar paintings moved back to the South of the Yangzhi river. "The four masters of the Wu School" nearby Su Zhou, namely Shen Zhou (1427–1509), Wen Zhengming (1470–1559), Tang Yin (1470–1523) and Qiu Ying (1493–1560) represented the highest level of scholar paintings of that period. In the late Ming Dynasty, the leading position of Wu School was replaced by the Huating School in Shanghai, with Mo Shilong (1539–1587) and Dong Qichang (1555–1636) as their representatives. The Wulin School in Hangzhou, or the Zhejiang School, represented by Daijin (1388–1462) and Lan Ying (1585–1664) was, to some extent, the continuation of the painting style of the South Song Dynasty represented by Ma Yuan. The school of painting was also unavoidably influenced by scholar paintings of the Yuan Dynasty. In the Ming Dynasty, there was a trend of exemplifying and formalizing the paintings of the Song and Yuan Dynasties. The scholar painters of the Song and Yuan Dynasties were against the formal painting style of the imperial art academy and considered it was skill of carvings and pattern of conventions. To them, paintings were merely the leisurely pursuit of brush works. Painters such as Su Shi painted only for fun, as well as to express his viewpoints, an experience or mean to seek the truth (*Dao*). After the development in the Yuan Dynasty, the scholar paintings of the Song Dynasty had accumulated enough classical works to form its own norms and system. Actually, the scholar painters just tried to copy and imitate the success of the ancient classical works. Calligraphers, painters and critics alike in the Ming Dynasty indicated that up to Mi Fu and his son in the Song Dynasty and the Four Masters of Yuan Dynasty, the development of paintings, as they knew it, would not go further. They thought their tasks were just to interpret and continue the works, the traditions, and the skills of the scholar paintings.

The meticulous and diverse painting styles of Shan Zhou and Wen Zhengming of the Wu School were the representative works of this period. Shen devoted his whole life to painting, poetry, literature and calligraphy. He was a professional scholar painter.

Fairy Land of Taoyuan (175cm×66.7cm), by Qiu Ying, collected by Tianjin Art Museum.

One of his two paintings currently in the procession of Taipei Palace Museum, *Lushan Mountain* (*Lushan Gao Tu*) looks majestic and grand, and full of diversity. The whole painting used texturing methods, a painting skill initiated by Wang Meng of the Yuan Dynasty. Obviously, the sole goal of the painting was to illustrate Wang Meng's painting skills and Shen Zhou did not use this method in any of his other paintings. The other, *Sitting at Night* (*Yezuo Tu*), shows an image of mountain at night with cottages at its foot and a man sitting by candle light. This time, Shen used a more steady and moist brushwork, a skill of Wu Zhen, another member of the "Four Masters of Yuan Dynasty." Shen kept the aloof, proud and seclusive style of Wu's. At the top of the painting, Shen wrote a prose of the same title (*Sitting at Night*) of more than 400 Chinese characters, making it as an integrated part of the painting, a perfect example of the practice to combine literature and calligraphy with painting at the time. The prose, with a refreshingly lucid style and full of implicit philosophic meanings, narrated the reflections of the painter while listening to the sound of nature in his cottage at night and demonstrated a harmony of "outside silence and inner tranquility", contrasting with the sounds and noises of the world at large. Shen even copied Dai Jin's works of his own period. Dai was a painter of Zhejiang School during Shen's time. We can only speculate: Shen accidentally read Dai's work and was inspired by his works and his endeavor to find a better way to follow and copy the paintings of previous generations. Wen Zhengming came from the same town as Shen, and he was a student of Shen during his youth. Both of them had no desire to become mandarins and were local celebrities who had mastered poetries, calligraphy and paintings. Wen mainly painted landscapes with thin and precise brushwork. He often used dark blue and green with a meticulous style of grace and elegance, full of lyric indications. His paintings of plum blossom and bamboo radiate bouquets of fresh and exquisite scent. Shen and Wen were alike in many aspects. They both came from wealthy families and shared a similar attitude to life of simplicity, and relatively uncomplicated experiences. A set of ideal attributes for them to enjoy the live as scholar painters.

Court ladies of Houshu Kingdom (124.7cm×63.6cm), by Tang Yin, collected by Beijing Palace Museum.

Compared with Shen Zhou and Wen Zhengming, Dong Qichang of a slight later period had a more aggressive style of art critics. Dong learned from the essences of Dong Yuan, Juran and Mi Fu of the Five Dynasties and the Northern Song Dynasty and Ni Zan and Huang Gongwang of the Yuan Dynasty and painted many vivid mountains, water, trees and stones. However Dong's position and influence in the fine art history were mainly from his proposal to divide Chinese paintings into the "north and south sects."

Dong Qichang, art name Xuanzai, was also known Sibai, or Xiangguang Jushi, and was born in Huating (now Songjiang County of Shanghai City). He was a successful candidate in the highest imperial examinations for mandarins and served as a minister. He was once appointed as the teacher to the crown prince. He was not only a famous artist, but also an important art connoisseur and collector. He collected many masterpieces of the "Four Masters of the Yuan Dynasty," including Huang Gongwang's *Living in Fuchun Mountain* (*Fuchun Shan Ju tu*), as well as Dong Yuan's work, which was already very rare at that time.

Scenery of Mountains in Lanrong scroll (138.8cm×53.3cm), by Dong Qichang, collected by Beijing Palace Museum.

Poetical Sense of Lin Hejing (154.1cm×64.3cm), by Dong Qichang, collected by Beijing Palace Museum.

He worked hard in painting and calligraphy. He also wrote many books to discuss theories of paintings and was a keen promoter of scholar paintings. His proposal that paintings could be divided into the north and south sects had a great influence to the development of fine art in China. It discussed in details the origins of different painting styles and the criteria to judge scholar painters. Mo Shilong, also from Huating, was the first to discuss the extension of north and south sects of Chinese Buddhism into his analysis of painting history. He wrote:

Buddhism was divided into north and south sects from the Tang Dynasty. Paintings were divided into south and north sects, also from the Tang Dynasty. However, painters should not be divided.

Paintings were divided into north and south sects, but the criteria to judge should not be based where painters came from and only related to the style of paintings. The north sect started from the imperial artist Li Sixun and his son in the Tang Dynasty and passed on to Ma Yuan and Xia Gui of the Imperial Art Academy in the Song Dynasty. South sect can be traced back to Wang Wei, a poet and artist of the Tang Dynasty, passing on to Dong Yuan of the Five Dynasties, Mi Fu of the Song Dynasty and to Huang Gongwang of the Yuan Dynasty. Mo Shilong was a close friend and a role model Dong Chichang had followed. They often exchanged views and shared many similar ideas. Dong followed Mo's assertion and further elaborated the development of scholar paintings:

Scholar paintings started from Wang Youcheng (Wang Wei) and were followed and developed by Dong Yuan, Seng Juran, Li Cheng and Fan Kuan. Li Longmian, Wang Jinqin (Wang Xian), Mi Nangong and Hu Er (Mi Fu and his son Mi Youren) learned from Dong and Ju, and then the tradition was passed on to the "Four Masters of Yuan Dynasty" of Huang Zijiu, Wang Shuming (Wang Meng), Ni Yuanzhen (Ni Zan) and Wu Zhonggui (Wu Zhen). Wen Zhengming and Shen Zhou of this dynasty inherited the style and the practice. However painters like Ma Yuan, Xia Gui, Li Tang and Liu Songnian followed the style of General Li and were different from that of ours.

Chen Jiru, another native from the same town as Dong Qichang continued:

Li school (Li Sixun and the north sect) was characterized with fine thin brushwork and did not have the fashion of scholars while the school of Wang (Wang Wei and his south sect) had the feature of Hui Neng and could not be followed by Shen Xiu.

The theory of south and north painting sects was spread widely because of Dong Qichang's influence. It controlled the development direction of scholar paintings in the Ming and Qing Dynasties, and provided for the first time a theoretic system to classify Chinese paintings, similar to that of Italian art and Netherlands art during the Renaissance in European. It appeared to be an objective way to classify Chinese paintings in accordance with their styles and techniques but Dong's inclination towards the southern sect was obvious. For him, south sect was equal to the scholar painting. Sudden awaking, scholarly spirit, and leisurely tranquility were all the virtues associated with the scholar paintings of the Southern Sect, a characteristic illustration of mandarins who were serving the court but longing for a seclusive life in the wide nature.

"Four Monks" and "Four Wangs"

During the reign of emperor Shun Zhi (1644–1661) to the early period of emperor Kang Xi (1662–1722) of the Qing Dynasty, the scholar paintings reached its peak of popularity and formed two distinctive directions of artistic pursuit. "Four Wangs" followed Dong Qichang's painting style, in pursuing coping ancient paintings as the goal of their endeavor, and were appreciated and favored by the imperial court. They were the school of orthodox. Another school, represented by the four monks and the Eight Masters of Jinling and Xin'an, consisted of many painters of the previous Ming Dynasty who escaped to the South. They had the spirit of exploration and innovation and used their landscapes to express their personnel feelings and political views.

"Four Monks" were Zhu Da, Shi Tao, Shi Xi and Hongren. At the end of the Ming Dynasty, Manchu entered into Beijing and established a unified Qing Dynasty, a repeat of the history of the late South Song Dynasty to the early Yuan Dynasty. Zhu Da and Shi Tao were descendants of the Ming Royalty and Shi Xi and Hongren considered they were the royal subjects of the Ming Dynasty. With a strong sense of nationalism, the four used their painting brushes to express their personnel feelings and their royalty to the fallen Ming Dynasty. In the art field, they insisted on innovation with continuality and rejected imitation without reasoning. They stressed on the importance of life experiences and paid special attentions to individual inspirations. They finally broke through the virtual fence of copying historical paintings and created a new era of paintings with bold and unique style. They not only injected vigor into the stagnant world of painting at that time, but also influenced the painters of future generations. Among them, Zhu Da and Shi Tao made the most important contributions.

Withered Wood and An Ichthyornis scroll (149.5cm×70cm), by Shi Tao, collected by Beijing Palace Museum.

Zhu Da (1626–1705), also known as Bada Shanren, was descendant of the previous imperial family and was brought up in a literary family. After the fall of the Ming Dynasty, he became a Buddhism monk and later a Taoist, entitling himself many vivid names among which were Bada Shanren, Xue Ge, Ge Shan, Yige Shan, Liang Yue and Dao Lang. He always expressed his emotions by his paintings through symbolism, implication and exaggeration. He often painted odd subjects in his paintings to express his cynical feelings and sadness on the fall of the Ming Dynasty. He used simple but bold brushwork with simple pattern,

Draft Paintings After Visiting Various Fantastic Mountains scroll (42.8cm×258.5cm), by Shi Tao, collected by Beijing Palace Museum.

perilous images and cool tone of compendious style. His landscape originated from Dong Yuan and modeled on Dong Qichang's pithy and elegant style with moist brushwork. Influenced by Lin Liang and Xu Wei of the Ming Dynasty, his flower-and-bird paintings had unique style of his own. On one piece of paper, he just painted one bird, or one fish, or one flower to create a sense of mystery. Bada Shanren also incorporated calligraphy skill into paintings, not only in brushwork, but also in outlining the whole image. Thus, his painting pattern was based on his control to abstract thinking. He was able to use ink to express virtually everything in the nature. It seemed that in his eye, birds, flowers and mountains were all black and white. He refused to use colors. To him, color was a kind of disturbance to his paintings. The strong symbolization of his paintings indicated his extreme feelings, including his curses and avoidance to the reality and condolence to the Ming Dynasty.

Shi Tao was also a descendant of the previous imperial family and he had frequent exchanges of letters with Zhu Da. They also cooperated in paintings but never met. They had the same reputation and appreciated each other. Shi Tao (1642–1707), originally surnamed Zhu, was entitled Yuan Ji after became a monk. He was also known as Shi Tao, Kugua Heshang, and Dadizi. Similar to Zhu Da, the sufferings brought by the overturn of the

Ming Dynasty and tragic personnel experiences always occupied a main position in the heart of this imperial descendant. He could only express his emotions through paintings. Shi Tao's landscapes modeled on various painters with unique style of thriving and refreshing images, and bold and new composition. His brushwork changed frequently in perilous but elegant pictures. His experience of traveling to different places greatly contributed to his paintings. He asserted to recreate all the mountains he visited in his paintings. He showed strong disregards to tradition. His paintings, no matter the cloud in the Huangshan Mountain, the river town in the South, the willows in the autumn, the pine trees along steep mountains, or the images of Lushan Mountain, and the scenery of Huanyin and Yangzhou, and Changshan, were artistic recreation of the original natural appearances. After Dong Qichang, copying ancient paintings had become a fashion and painters like Shi Tao, who painted subjects directly from the nature, was very rare. Nowadays, there are still many of Shi Tao's work survived, among which were *Voice of the Mountains and Waters* (*Shanshui Qingyin*), *Xiyuan Elegant Paintings Album* (*Xiyuan Yatu Ji*), *Autumn of Huaiyin and Yangzhou* (*Huaiyang Jieqiu Tu*), *Album of the Eight Wonders in Huangshan Mountain* (*Huangshan Basheng Ce*), *Paintings of Visiting Lushan Mountain* (*Lushan Youlan Tu*) and *Watching Mountains in Yuhang* (*Yuhang Kanshan Tu*).

Picture Album of Plucking Water Chestnuts, by Jin Nong, collected by Beijing Palace Museum.

Shi Xi (date of birth unknown and religious name Kun Can) and Hong Ren (1610–1661 with religious name of Jianjiang Heshang) were known as two "painter monks." They considered themselves as the subjects of the Ming Dynasty. They had less resentments but more detached attitudes compared with Zhu Da and Shi Tao. Shi Xi's painting style of landscapes was modeled on the paintings of Wang Meng and Huang Gongwang. His paintings of landscape were drawn by copying the real sceneries. Painted with texturing methods, his paintings were generous but not rigid, with magnificent and vast scales of views. Hong Ren followed Ni Zan's painting style in landscapes. He often painted famous mountains, especially Huangshan, and was a representative of the "Xin'an Family."

Just like "Four Masters of Yuan Dynasty" who were universally respected in the Ming and Qing Dynasties, "Four Monks" of the late Ming and the early Qing Dynasties and their painting styles were highly appreciated by painters and collectors at the present time. Historian of fine art Wang Bomin commented Four Monks' paintings, "their paintings consisted of thick atmosphere of Buddhism and Taoism thinking. They often combined their different emotions such as sadness and resentments together in their paintings. In general, their paintings were simple. In history, Confucians valued a simple style and preferred tranquility and simplicity. Just as the old saying, 'white jade without carving and polishing is valueless.' In case of their specific differences in paintings, Hong Ren won for his elegance and unconventionally free brushwork; Kun Can won for his honesty painting style and steady brushwork; Bada Shanren won for his romantic charm and simply brushwork; and Shi Tao won for his boldness and unrestrained brushwork. During a period when most painters intend to copy ancient paintings, they broke the trend and demonstrated their unique paintings to the world. This is very unusual in history."

"Four Wangs" refers to Wang Shimin (1592–1680, art name Xun Zhi and also called Yan Ke, and Luxi Laoren, born in Taicang, Jiangsu Province), Wang Jian (1598–1677), (also called Xiang Bi and Ranxiang Anzhu, born also in Taicang), Wang Hui (1632–1717, art name Shigu, and also called Ken Yan Shang Ren, born in Changshu, Jiangsu Province) Wang Yuanqi (1642–1715, art name Mao Jing, and also called Lu Tai). Together with Wu Li and Yun Ge (1633–1690, art name Shou Ping, and also called Nan Tian, born in Changzhou Jiangsu), they were collectively known as "Four Wangs and Wu and Yun" or "Six Masters of the Early Qing Dynasty." They all accepted Dong Qichang's theory of art as infallible laws and devoted themselves to copy ancient paintings. They stressed on brushwork skills and sought a mild style. The "Four Wangs" had outstanding social positions. They traveled extensively and had a large numbers of students with great influences among the officials. Their styles were appreciated by the imperial court and thus were regarded as orthodox school with influences until the modern age.

The most common comments on "Four Wangs" are they had solid foundation for brushwork and had developed unique painting composition and rhythm. However, since they neglected the observation to the nature and disrespected the personal experiences of the nature, most of their paintings were monotonous and lethargic, and lacking of new concepts and directions. This prevented them from making greater achievements. Actually, what the four Wangs had achieved was to elevate the academic study of ancient paintings to an unprecedented level of height, though such academic study relied very much on personal preferences. What interested to "Four Wangs," were Dong Yuan and Juran of the Five Dynasties, Li Cheng, Fan Kuan, Guo Xi, Mi Fu and his son, Zhao Boju and Wang Shen of the Northern Song and Zhao Mengfu and "Four Masters of Yuan Dynasty", all of whom belonged to the "Southern Sect" as denoted by Dong Qichang. Wang Bomin pointed out that the studies of four Wangs on the paintings of "Southern Sect" lasted for more than a century and their pious attitudes alone deserved respect. Just like Chinese scholars treasured the teachings of the wise ancestors, Chinese painters also believed that the true essence of landscapes should be illustrated with equally perfect language. Often the painters during the Ming and Qing period would write to claim to have copied ancient painters on their paintings, just to reflect their modesty and their respect to the general fashion of the time. They did not really blindly follow ancient painters. One typical example is that even Shi Tao and Bada Shanren, painters with strong personal style, sometime would say they were just copying some ancient painters in the postscripts. Surely, no one believes.

The End of Scholar Paintings and Famous Chinese Painters of Modern Times

Yangzhou Eight Eccentrics" of the mid Qing Dynasty should be considered as the last masters of Chinese scholar paintings. From the reigns of Jia Qing (1796–1820) and Dao Guang of the Qing Dynasty (1821–1850) to the early 20th century, the traditional society had gradually been on the decline. As a result of the social transformation, the cultural environment that traditional scholars lived on also disappeared rapidly. The western influence advanced eastwards with vengeance and to the extend and at the speed which were never experienced by that of Buddhism more than 1,000 years ago. Inevitably there was a great change in the field of paintings. Scholar paintings and imperial paintings gradually declined. Shanghai and Guangzhou, two trading ports, became the new center of paintings with "Hai Sect" and "Lingnan Sect" as the representatives of the new era. Hai means overseas in Chinese. "Hai Sect" combined traditional Chinese styles with the newly arrived western painting skills.

"Yangzhou Eight Eccentrics", or "Yangzhou Painting Sect" referred to a group of scholar painters in Yangzhou in the middle 18th century, including Jin Nong, Huang Shen, Zhen Xie, Li Shan, Li Fangying, Luo Pin, Hua Yan, Gao Fenghan, Min Zhen, Bian Shoumin and several others. "Yangzhou Eight Eccentrics" all showed strong personality in their paintings. Their attitudes towards painting traditions were in a clear contrast to that of "Four Wangs and Wu and Yun". They seldom copied paintings of the

Seals in Painting and Calligraphic Works

Since the Ming and Qing Dynasties, seals have become an integral part of painting and calligraphic works. A well-round painter is expected to be well-versed in painting and calligraphic theories, have a thorough knowledge of painting, calligraphic and carving techniques, and highly skilled in these techniques. Most famous painters are not only adept at painting but also good at carving seals which complement their paintings and form a unity with their paintings. Seals in paintings and calligraphic works are mostly seals carved by the painters and calligraphers themselves, seals of the prefacers, and seals of the collectors and appraisers. Seals typically feature regular names, style names, verses, auspicious words, mottos, and collection and appraisal marks.

so called "South Sect". Instead, they followed the style of Shi Tao and regard Xu Wei and Bada Shanren as their artistic guardians. "Yangzhou Eight Eccentrics" were not good at painting landscape. Painting birds, flowers, plum blossoms and bamboos was their specialty. They often considered themselves to be blossoming plum, orchid, bamboo and chrysanthemum. The four flowers have, in the traditional Chinese view, scholarly characteristics. During the reign of Qian Long (1736–1795) of the Qing Dynasty, Yangzhou was a prosperous consumer city with strong trading activities. Many of these scholars made a living by selling their paintings and calligraphy. Compared with carefully organized landscapes, flower-and-bird paintings were more suitable to illustrate the beauty of freehand brushwork, and painters could paint with fewer simple strokes, to radiate the elegance of Chinese characters.

Of the "Yangzhou Eight Eccentrics," Jin Nong (1687–1764, also called Dongxin Xiansheng) and Zheng Xie (Zheng Banqiao) were considered to possess the most typical scholarly characteristics. Jin Nong lived in poverty all his life and was very cynical towards the society. He liked traveling and had been to many famous mountains. It was said that he only started to learn painting in his 50s. At the beginning he learnt the style of Wen Tong of the Song Dynasty and Wang Mian of the Yuan Dynasty and gradually developed his signature style of simplicity which was called the "Jin Nong Style." He often painted flowers with light ink, plum blossoms with tilted branches. Occasionally, he also painted landscape and people with unique rhythm and personality. Zheng Banqiao served as a low-rank official. He alienated the authority when he insisted to apply for emergency relieves for people in a natural disaster. He resigned and went to Yangzhou. He made a living by painting and selling paintings. Like Bada Shanren and Shi Tao, he used paintings to express his personnel resentment and to illustrate his lofty social attitude and moral sanity against a background of corruption and importance. Also, he painted only with ink and his signature compositions were orchids and

A Lady, colored on paper, by Ren Bonian, collected by Nanjing Museum.

bamboos. His paintings have very strong visual effect. However, in the eyes of traditional scholars, these paintings lack inner exquisite grace.

Painters in China's trading port Shanghai were considered to belong collectively to "Hai Sect." Some of the painters' scopes went beyond the traditional scholar paintings, with Zhao Zhiqian (1829–1884), Ren Bonian (1840–1896), Wu Youru (1840–1893) and Wu Changshuo (1844–1927) as their typical representatives. During this period, scholars no longer had rich families to support them and did not enjoy the high social status they used to. They had fallen to become one of the craftsman or artisan painters that they so often look down upon. Zhao Zhiqian barely supported a living by selling his paintings. Thus, he could not appreciate invaluable ancient calligraphies and paintings as Dong Qichang did. His

Portrait of Painer Gao Yi (130.9cm× 48.5cm), by Ren Bonian, collected by Shanghai Museum.

flower-and-bird paintings would have to meet the demands of aesthetic standard required by his clients but he still endeavored to continue the tradition and scholarly standard of grace and elegance. Compared with his predecessors in the early Qing Dynasty and the late Ming Dynasty, Zhao's paintings were more meticulous and lucidly colorful with present compositions, to the enjoyment of both secular society and scholar circle Ren Bonian used to be an apprentice in a fan-painting workshop. He was not a very traditional scholar by any standard, but he was a rising talented young artist, and he was especially an excellent portrait and flower-and-bird painter. Ren Bonian painted with light and graceful ink strokes and went beyond most imperial court painters in terms of accuracy, meticulousness, and radiance and clarity. He painted carefully each piece of single flower, grass, feather, insect and fish. His portrait paintings were the world first class, and accurately and gracefully depicted the subjects. Wu Youru was the first person who transformed the Chinese traditional paintings into a modern industry. In the 10th year of reign of Guang Xu period (1884), he was employed as the editor in chief and chief painter of *Dianshizhai Huabao* (Painting Supplement), a supplement of *Shenbao* (Shanghai News). For more than a decade, he published more than 4,000 paintings in the newspaper he edited. He reported news with articles supported with the traditional Chinese line drawings. He also painted many pictures of foreign lands such as trains, buildings, ships, gunboats and off course the people, which were welcomed and liked by common people. Like Ren Bonian, Wu Changshuo was also a career painter, but with more profound literary background.

Before he took up painting brush, he served as the first president of Xileng Yinshe, a very famous art society in Hangzhou. Wu Changshuo was a student of Ren Bonian, but his painting style was influenced to a great extend by Zhao Zhiqian and Chen Chun, Xu Wei, Badashan Ren, Shi Tao and "Yangzhou Eight Eccentric." Wu Changshuo's achievement in calligraphy helped his painting greatly. He was good at writing different style of calligraphy with soft brush pens made of sheep hair and with the inspiration he had gained he painted many different subjects with each unique type of brush strokes, the strength and elasticity of Lishu (an official script style of calligraphy developed in the Han Dynasty) and Zhuanshu (a style of Chinese calligraphy often used on seals) in the paintings of branches and climbs and the vibrancy and enthusiasm of Xingshu (running hand in Chinese calligraphy) and *Caoshu* (cursive script in Chinese calligraphy) in the paintings of chrysanthemums and grapes. He went beyond Zhao Zhiqian in using colors. He studied and adopted many techniques used in the Chinese folk and western paintings. He constantly mixed red, yellow and green into reddish brown to seek a sense of harmony in conflicts.

What happened to "Hai Sect" and other paintings of the late Qing Dynasty demonstrated clearly a society in change and the associated trend of art in general and paintings in particular. The scholar era had surely and definitely ended. With the abolishing of imperial examination system, traditional scholars did not have any hope to become officials and theoretically they would only be common people all their lives. Their dreams of living in seclusion through scholar paintings seemed so ridiculous that they had to live in a social seclusion daily and permanently. However, the aesthetic standard of the scholar paintings developed over thousand years of the imperial history had become part of this nation and still had a place in the society. Painters did not abandon their hope and this aesthetic standard simply because of the social changes. The legacy of the scholar paintings lived on through the papers and brush strokes which once served for their purposes.

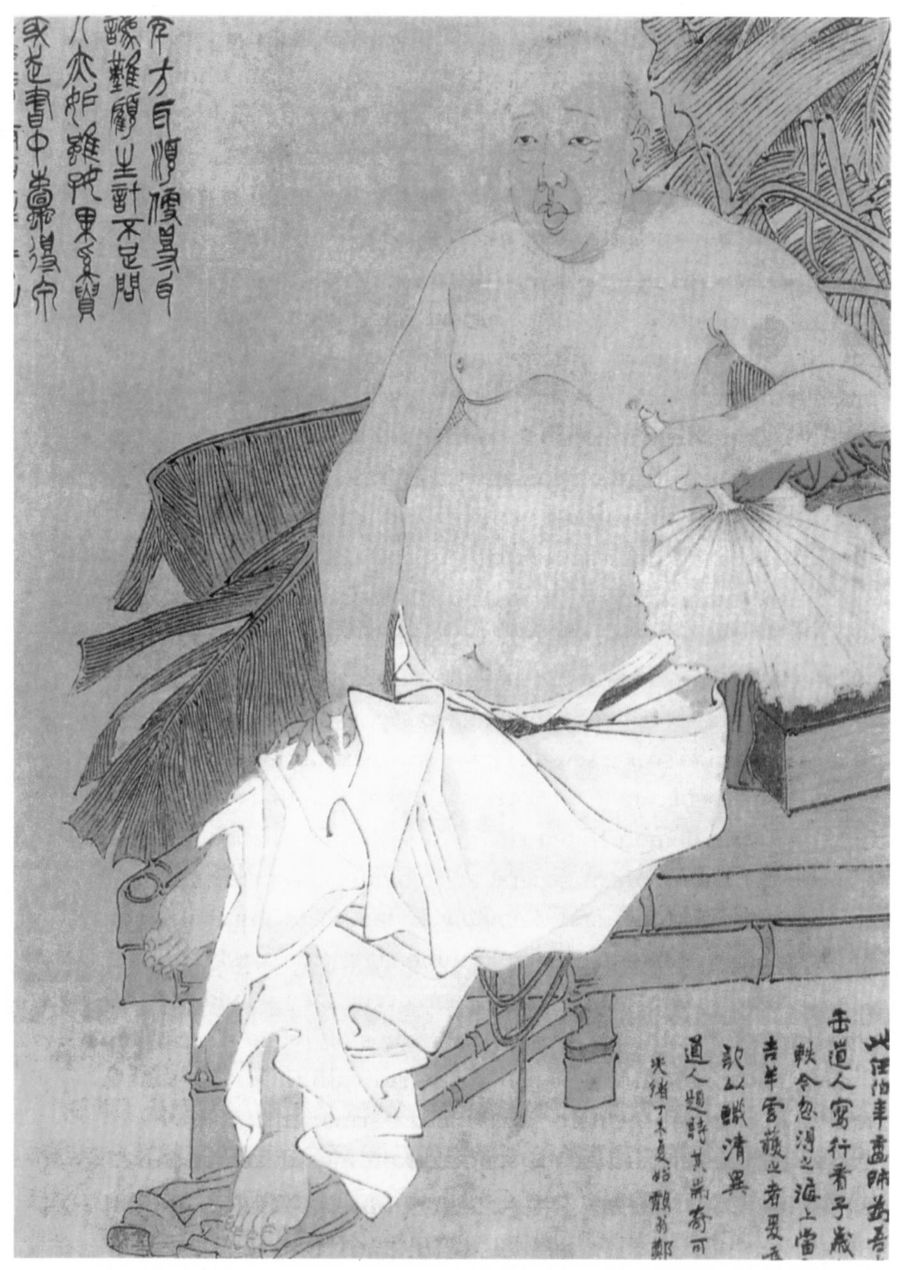

Enjoying the Cool Under Banana Trees scroll, Wu Changshuo's Portrait by Ren Bonia, part, collected by Nanjing Museum.

These paintings were closely connected with the emotions of the Chinese people and the approaches of how they experienced nature and the world. When a Chinese and a foreign come across the term of "Chinese painting," their comprehension may entirely be different. The latter may think it refers to all the paintings in China while the former knows clearly that it only refers to those that follow the style of ancient paintings, and the paintings done by traditional scholar painters. When oil painting arrived in China from the West, it and its associated style had a great influence to the paintings of China. It is therefore necessary to keep the concept of "Chinese painting", a term to comprise all those characteristics of the traditional aesthetics and ways of expressions for the sake of historical continuality.

Many painters in the 20th century still practiced the traditional painting style and many of them have become celebrity great masters of the traditional Chinese painting. However the society in which the modern painters lived is far more complicated than that of their predecessors. Although the society in general still accept the notion that "Chinese styles as the fundamental structures, the Western skills for practical uses," the traditional Chinese painters" still have to face many challenges of the increasingly influential western culture and its associated values and they need to readjust themselves to meet the new roles they will play in a society where the traditional Chinese values are gradually eroding their dominant position. As dissolute with the painting style of the four Wangs' in the imitation of every thing which was old, some painters tried to create new painting approaches and to look for inspirations from art heritages other than the scholar paintings, such as the Dunhuang murals and the folk arts. But all these endeavors failed to become the mainstream of Chinese painting. The concept and format of the scholar painting actually have become an integrated part of the "Chinese national culture," the thoughts of the Confucius, Mencius, Laozi and Zhuangzi. It ever has gained the title of the "national painting" during the

Sights From a Boat on Shujiang River (76.5cm×48cm), by Huang Binhong, collected by Nanjing Museum.

process, and its rise and fall are closed linked with the fortune of the "national culture." In the first half of the 20th century, China experienced the collapse of the last imperial dynasty, the civil wars of warlords, the establishment of the Republic of China, the war against Japanese invasion, the civil war between Communist Party and Nationalist Party, the establishment of the People's Republic of China and many political movements therefore after. Despite of all these great social, political, and cultural changes, a large number of great masters of Chinese traditional painting emerged. They had profound conscious of the national culture values and their paintings had kept certain distances to the modern thoughts and aesthetic concepts. They, inevitably to some extent were influenced by the experiences and emotions of the modern society. In this very challenging time, they responded spontaneously to shoulder the responsibilities to transform China's traditional painting. They tried to combine the tradition with the modern reality. Their resolution and determination to face all the external challenges and to create a modern style of their own are inspirational.

Qi Baishi (1863–1957) from Hunan Province reminded us Wang Mian of the Yuan Dynasty and Jin Nong of the "Yangzhou Eight Eccentrics." Actually, they were admired by Qi Baishi. Other favorite painters of his included Xu Wei, Shi Tao, Zhu Da, Li Chan of "Yangzhou Eight Eccentrics," and Wu Changshuo of the "Hai Sect." Most importantly, he had worked as a carpenter. His experience and inspiration as a folk artist is very unique. Qi Baishi was very diligent artist and lived a long life. Critics say Qi Baishi only completed the prefect combination of the aptitude of the rural poets and the style of the scholar painting at the age of 70. His paintings belonged to the scholar painting, but not exactly. You could smell the fragrance of the rural life in his paintings, in a sharp contrast to dusty scent of scholarly museum in a scholar painting. Qi Baishi's freehand brushworks in his late years were rustic rather than unrestrained with the traces of innocence and vibrancy of a rural carpenter. His paintings are full of the sights and sounds

Picture of My Jieshan Yinguan Study (one of mountains-and-waters scrolls) (128cm×62cm) colored on paper, by Qi Baishi,1932, collected by Chongqing Museum.

Tumbler (Bu Dao Weng) (128cm×33cm), colored on paper, by Qi Baishi, 1926, collected by China Art Gallery.

of the rural life. Frogs croak, cicadas, crops, chicks, locusts and even daily family utensils have become vivid subjects of his paintings. His masterpieces include *Corns and Dragonflies* (*Yumi Qingting*) and *Washang Shili* (*Loud Frog Croak*). Traditionally scholar painters would use light color to depict a lofty grace. But Qi Baishi painted red flowers and dark green leaves with heavy visual impacts. Huang Binhong (1865–1955) was a master painter who learnt early but matured late. He had a totally different style to that of Qi Baishi. Huang Binhong had a well educated background and shared a similar attitude towards study to that of the "Four Wangs." He devoted almost entirely his youth into studying and imitating ancient paintings. He inherited the tradition of the painters of the Song and Yuan Dynasties towards the nature. He visited many mountains and rivers in China. He completed his endeavor to transform his brushwork at the age of 80 and became a great master of fine art.

Plum Blossoms and Rocks (127cm×67cm),by Wu Changshuo, 1902, collected by Hangzhou Xiling Publishing House

Pan Tianshou (1897–1971) and Fu Baoshi (1904–1965) were two geniuses of painting. Wang Bomin commented on Pan Tianshou's paintings: "People usually use 'depth, weight and grand' as the criterions to judge a painting during the period of the Republic. Pan Tianshou's paintings were perfect to meet all these criterions, especially 'grand'." Even he painted small piece of sketch, and you feel grand. The "grand" does not refer to the size of the paintings, but refer to his style of "solid frames" or "solid bones", depicting the power and force of his brushwork." "Strong bones and empty minds" is a tradition of Taoist, meaning person should have strong bones to carry his duties but empty minds to have no worries. Pan Tianshou had the honesty and simplicity of a common farmer

Picture of Pines, Rocks, Plum Blossom and the Moon (329cm×149cm), by Pan Tianshou, collected by Pan Tianshou Museum.

and the culture and wisdom of a well educated scholar. He combined the painting styles of both the "Northern Sect" and "Southern Sect," which deviated from but improve the gentle and exquisite approach of flower-and-bird paintings of the Ming and Qing Dynasties and created a painting style of force and strength. Flower and bird, and bamboo and stone were the main composition of his paintings. It had the structure and rigidness of sculpture but yet still radiating with refreshing tranquility of morning mist. Fu Baoshi admired Shi Tao tremendously and even changed his name from Ruiling into Baoshi. He liked painting after drinking alcohol and was a romantic artist with poetic quality. He went to Japan to study western paintings and was good at commanding color palettes. His landscapes were very vibrant and full of expressions. His figure painting skill could be compared to Gu Kaizhi of the Eastern Jin Dynasty. His masterpieces include *Nine Songs* (*Jiu Ge*) and *Walking with Beauty* (*Liren Xing*). Pan Tianshou and Fu Baoshi, though their paintings still belonged to the scholar painting conceptually, had paved a way for the modern Chinese paintings to prosper.

Modern Chinese Paintings

Painters Studying Abroad

Portrait of Bright and Virtuous High-Level Imperial Concubine, oil painting on paper, by Giuseppe Castiglione, Qing Dynasty, collected by Beijing Palace Museum.

In 1601, Italian missionary Matteo Ricci came to China and brought with him some European paintings. His gifts for emperor Shenzong of the Ming Dynasty (1573–1619) included oil paintings of God and Madonna. Many Chinese painters were surprised at the vivid resemblance but they were not highly appreciated and Chinese painters did not follow the painting style. In the early Qing Dynasty, many European missionaries came to China and many of them could paint in oil. They worked in the imperial court, including Italian artists Joseph Castiglione, S.J. (1688–1766), Joseph Panzi (1733–1812) and French painter Jean-Denis Attiret (1702–1768). They were the first group of foreign painters to serve at the Chinese imperial court and were asked to paint portraits. Emperor Qianlong chose several young servants to learn oil painting from them.

After the Opium War, China's exchanges with foreign countries became more frequent. More western religious and commercial paintings arrived in China, exerting more influence to the traditional Chinese paintings. But it was not until late 19th century that China had painters who really mastered the western painting skill. During the reign of Tongzhi (1862–1874), several missionaries from French established an orphanage in Shanghai and taught them various skills, one of which was oil painting. After these orphans grew up, they passed the oil painting skill they learnt to the society. In the late Qing Dynasty and early Republic of China, Zhou Xiang, Zhang Yuguang and Xu Yongqing, who were very active in Shanghai, were all from this orphanage.

Meanwhile, some Chinese scholars went to Europe to study and see the outstanding paintings with their own eyes. Xue Fucheng (1838–1894) who served as ambassadors to Britain, France, Italy and Belgium in the late Qing Dynasty wrote the book *Visiting Oil Paintings* in Paris describing his experience of visiting a waxwork museum and oil painting museum in Paris, and became a very popular book. The modern political activist and philosopher Kang Youwei (1858–1927) also highly appreciated the paintings of Italian Renaissance in his article a *Journey to Italy*. Through their introductions, Chinese intellects, for the first time, understood another kind of painting skill which was totally different to that of Chinese paintings.

The newly arrived painting interested many Chinese painters and they started to try painting in oil from books and publications and explored various alternative pigments. They still painted oil paintings with Chinese traditional style. The situation did not change until the youths who studied abroad came back. Li Tiefu (1869–1952) was one of those who went abroad to learn oil painting. He went to the United States in 1887 and was taught by J. S. Sargent (1856–1925). Li Shutong went to Japan to learn painting and came back to China in 1910. On his return, he taught in Tianjin, Hangzhou and Nanjing. He initiated the practice of coping statue and to draw pictures from real human models. He also organized painting society in the universes to study the western paintings.

After the Revolution of 1911, more Chinese went abroad to study western painting, mainly to Europe, the United States and Japan, and they included Li Yishi, Feng Gangbai, Wu Fading, Li Chaoshi, Fang Junbi, Lin Fengmian, Xu Beihong, Pan Yuliang, Zhou

Traditional Prints in Folk Arts

The development of China's traditional prints is closely related to the engraving industry. The centers of traditional prints in the Song and Yuan Dynasties were Jian'an in Fujian and Hangzhou in Zhejiang, and shifted to Nanjing and Beijing in the Ming Dynasty. Yet, traditional prints didn't enter a new phase of development until the rise of the Huizhou school of prints. As early as the 15th century, the Huizhou school of prints was noted for its printing and numerous highly skilled artists, especially those from the Huang and Wang families. In the Ming and Qing Dynasties, the Huang family in Xin'an produced more than 200 volumes of prints; it had more than 100 members skilled in the prints. This sizable team of print artists produced representative works such as Cultivating Rectitude: Illustrated and Explained and Legend of Ancient Women of Virtue. While the Huizhou school of prints was all the rage for its elegant and elaborate style, prints in Jinling (Nanjing), Wulin (Hangzhou) and Suzhou developed their own characteristics.

New Year Pictures in Folk Arts
Wooden printed New Year pictures emerged in the late Ming Dynasty and grew and expanded in the early Qing Dynasty, with a number of production centers springing up across the nation. The centers had strong production capacity and marketed their products across vast geographic regions. They featured prominent local characteristics and the most famous ones included Yangliuqing in Tianjin, Taohuawu in Suzhou, and Yangjiabu in Shandong's Wei County. New Year picture workshops emerged at Yangliuqing in the west of Tianjin during the Reign of Emperor Wan Li of the Ming Dynasty and thrived in the Reign of Qianlong of the Qing Dynasty; shortly afterwards, Yangliuqing became a major center of New Year pictures in northern China. Yangliuqing New Year pictures covered a wide range of subject matters, including mythology, local customs, historical tales, operas, novels, babies, and beauties. They had strong drawing effects and are made with single-color plates and manual coloring. Due to their elaborate workmanship and bright colors, they sold briskly in northern, northeastern and northwestern China. Taohuawu was home to the largest cluster of arts and crafts businesses in northern Suzhou. In Taohuawu, New Year pictures can date back to the Ming Dynasty. New Year picture workshops emerged in the reign of Emperor Kangxi of the

Bichu, Pang Xunqin, Yan Wenliang, Chang Shuhong, Lv Sibai, Wu Zuoren, Tang Yihe, Zhou Fangbai, Wu Guanzhong, Wu Dayu, Zhao Wuji and Zhu Dequn. When Chinese students first went to West Europe, impressionistic and post impressionistic painting had gained prominent popularity and the influence of classical paintings of academicism was gradually reduced. Li Yishi, Wu Fading, Li Chaoshi, Xu Beihong, Yan Wenliang and Chang Shuhong who studied in Europe promoted the realism classical painting. In Japan, new painting movement, represented by Kuroda Seiki (1866–1924), had changed Japan's fine art education with the introduction of the impressionism. Wang Yuezhi, Chen Baoyi, Hu Gentian, Yu Jifan, Feng Zikai, Chen Zhifo, Fu Baoshi, Wang Jiyuan, Guan Liang, Xu Xingzhi, Ni Yide, Wei Tianlin and Wang Shikuo all had been to Japan. Since Japan did not have profound oil painting tradition as France, those studied in Japan tended to follow various trends of impressionism. After they came back to China, they usually taught in schools to pass on their painting skills and its associated concept of art.

Xu Beihong (1895–1953), Liu Haisu (1896–1994) and Lin Fengmian (1900–1990) were painters and educators of fine art who had studied abroad. They were famous oil painter as well as masters of Chinese painting in the 20th century, with profound influences to the formation and development of China's modern painting. In 1912, Liu Haisu established Shanghai Academy of Drawing and Art at the age of 17. In 1919, the academy was renamed as Shanghai School of Fine Art. This was the first institution of higher education in Chin's formal art education history. In 1920s China's first national art school, National Beiping School of

Art, China's first art university college, Hangzhou National University College of Art and Department of Fine Art, Nanjing Central University and Suzhou School of Fine Art were also established successively. Xu Beihong, Liu Haisu, Lin Fengmian and Yan Wenliang (1893–1988) taught in these institutions, and their unique individual artistic understanding brought different characteristics to these schools.

Xu Beihong was trained in the tradition of academism in Paris and was a painter of realism. He insisted profoundly on the training of sketch drawing and the precision of perspectives. He strongly believed the first objective of art was realism and real life was the source of art. The other major contribution he made was his effort to improve Chinese traditional painting skill by integrating with that of the western classical realism. On the other hand, he also tried to use the elements of person emotions of Chinese paintings in his oil paintings. Similar to Li Shutong, (1880–1942) a master of poet, calligraphy and painting, Xu Beihong's oil paintings were full of Chinese characteristics though he used the traditional western painting techniques. In their endeavor to master the western painting techniques, the two painters did not disregard their qualities as Chinese traditional scholars. In his paintings of *Yugong Moves Mountains* and *Jiu Fang Gao*, though painted with ink and Xuan paper, Xu used real persons as models and the paintings illustrated strong characteristics of academicism art. These two paintings had inspired a tremendous interest in the field of art which were so used to the scholar paintings. His paintings of galloping horses were also caused a similar response. Different to pet horses in Han Gan's paintings of

Qing Dynasty, and boomed in the reigns of Emperors Yongzheng and Qianlong of the Qing Dynasty. Taohuawu's New Year pictures mostly featured tales and depict cityscapes and resident's life. They were made with chromatic wood carving methods, as well as a shading technique developed during the reign of Emperor Qianlong of the Qing Dynasty. They were realistic, brilliant, and conspicuous. Yangjiabu, located in the northeastern of Shandong's Wei County, saw rapidly expanding New Year picture production in the reign of Emperor Qianlong and flourishing production in the reign of Emperor Tongzhi of the Qing Dynasty. Yangjiabu New Year pictures mostly featured mythology and a wide variety of subject matters. They are printed primarily with separate color sheet-works. They had dramatic designs, full and ornamental composition, strongly contrasting colors, and simplistic and vivid styles. Zhuxian Town in Henan, Fengxiang in Shaanxi, Mianzhu in Sichuan, Quanzhou in Fujian, and Foshan in Guangdong also produced New Year pictures of unique styles. New Year pictures declined in the late Qing Dynasty with the spread of Western lithography to China.

Silent Valley (269cm×90cm), by Zhang Daqian, 1965.

the Tang Dynasty, the horses under Xu Beihong's brushes were very sporty and muscular. Obviously, he was a master of anatomy. Liu Haisu, who was one year younger than Xu Beihong, went to France in 1930s. The painters which interested him most were those of classical art with romantic spirit and post-impressionistic painters in the European history of fine art. He was enthusiastically imitating paintings of Titian, Rembrandt, Eugène Delacroix, van Gogh and Paul Cezanne. But he still showed his tolerance to embrace arts of different schools in his later paintings and teachings. Liu Haisu's paintings completed after he came back to China were considered to be the masterpieces in Chinese oil painting history. His splash-ink and splash-color paintings were the final expression of his sensitivity to painting trends and his character of daring to be the first, rather than a return to the tradition of random scholar painting. Lin Fengmian learnt painting in the fine art schools in Dijon and Paris of France. He was influence by paintings of academism and impressionism and fauvism. He devoted all his life to find a way to integrate Chinese and western painting skills and all his paintings could be regarded as his experiments in this regard. Most of his paintings in his middle and later years were painted on Xuan paper, but none of them was painted only using the traditional scholar painting skill. Color and form had become the theme of his paintings and elements of western skills played important supporting roles. Almost each of his paintings used characteristic elements of Chinese paintings, such as maids of imperial palace, characters of drama, and elements of landscape and flower-and-bird paintings. The final results were Chinese ink

Music of A Vertical Bamboo Flute, oil painting (48cm×35cm), by Xu Beihong, 1926.

Naked Woman, oil painting, by Lin Fengmian, 1934.

paintings with western characteristics, an organic blend of Chinese calligraphic lines and western formalism.

Revolutionary Realism

In 1920s and 1930s, many Chinese painters who shared a common interest formed groups and launched various activities. Pang Xunqin (1906–1985) established the Jue Lan Society in 1932, to promote and introduce western modern paintings to the general public; China Independent Fine Art Association established by Chinese students trained in Japan promoted the neorealist paintings. However, these associations failed to make significant impact as they were only active in a limited space and time in Shanghai. During the first national fine art exhibition in early 1929, the argument between Xu Beihong and Xu Zhimo on the assessments of western modern painters indicated the contradiction of fine artists' values at that period of time. Xu Beihong denounced impressionism and fauvism paintings, calling paintings of Renoir, Cezanne and Matisse

being shameless. Xu Zhimo argued strongly for these painters to reinstall their position and value in the history of fine art. Judging from oil painters at that time, more painters chose to learn paintings after impressionism and few studied classical oil painting. The number of painters who really mastered classical painting skill was rare.

After the war broke out against Japanese invasion, Chinese painters took up their paintings as weapons to assist the war effort. Painters with different artistic views put their difference aside and jointed the war effort as a united force. They, like many other ordinary people, lost home and began a life of refuges. They experienced the joys and sorrows of the society. They went to the remote areas in the northwest and southwest China which were still under the rule of the Nationalists. The new experience and life inspired them to find new emotional dimensions. They were accumulating ideas and reserving energies for the new functions of arts. Many experiments of new forms and movements of fine art started before the war stopped. Many painters who were involved changed their style to make a contribution to the society in drawing propaganda paintings of realism to aid the anti-Japanese aggression movement. Xu Beihong wrote, anti-Japanese aggression war had promoted China's realism painting and he expressed his happiness that so many new painting movements had disappeared during the war. After Japan was defeated, modernists emerged again. In 1945, Lin Fengmian, Ni Yide, Guan Liang, Li Zhongsheng, Yu Feng, Zhao Wuji and Yu Yanyong held the first exhibition of the Independent Fine Art Association. However, the effort to rejuvenate the new art movements was very short lived and their activities stopped in 1949. Although the realism painting and the Taoist concept of using art to promote *Dao* (the way or the truth) had dominated the field of art, the noble art either the traditional scholar paintings or the western classical paintings seemed not to be appropriate in a time of war.

Wood engraving which was easy to make with lucid presentations was very popular in China from 1920s to

Galloping Horse (95cm×68cm), ink and wash on paper, by Xu Beihong, 1939, collected by Xu Beihong Museum.

< up *Such a Beautiful Landscape* (65cm×30.2cm), by Fu Baoshi, 1959, Private collection.
< down *Poetical Sense of Mao Zedong* (46.3cm×58.4cm), by Fu Baoshi, 1962, collected by Nanjing Museum.

Tian Heng and Five Hundred Rebels (198cm×355cm), oil painting on canvas, 1928-1930, collected by Xu Beihong Museum.

1940s. The greatest novelist and art critic in the 20th century, Lu Xun (1881–1936) was an active promoter of Chinese modern wood engravings. Under his Influence, many bright and vigorous young artists gathered in Shanghai, the cultural and artistic center of China then and devoted themselves to the New Culture Movement. Wood engravings in Shanghai during 1930s followed the western style because of the influence of German expressionism promoted by Lu Xun. To many angry young Chinese painters, the paintings of German woman artist Kathe Kollwitz's (1867–1945) represented the voices and images of the international proletarians and revolutionists beyond the national boundaries. The early works of Li Hua (1907–1944), Jiang Feng (1910–1982) and Huang Xinbo (1916–1980) showed their efforts in seeking an internationally and mutually understandable language. On June 2, 1932, Chundi Fine Art Institute, established by the members of Fine Artist Left-wing Alliance held a wood engraving exhibition in Shanghai and many German engravings collected by Lu Xun made their appearance to the public.

In 1942, the Chinese Communist Party leader, Mao Zedong, published the famous article, *A lecture note in Yan'an on Literature and Art*. He proposed that literature and art should serve the politics, serve the revolution and the war effort and serve workers, peasants and soldiers,

Huangshan Mountain, oil painting, by Lin Fengmian, 1980s.

and literature and art to be subject to the revolutionary requirements stipulated by the Communist Party of China during each specific period of time. Mao Zedong's talk exerted great influences, and was spread nationwide through various channels. During the war against Japanese invasion, many progressive intellectuals, including those left-wing wood engraving artists in Shanghai, gathered in Yan'an from various parts of China. During the time of war and revolution, Chinese traditional painting had lost its popularity, especially those scholar paintings that advocate deliberate brushworks. Under the arduous environment of the Shaanxi-Gansu-Ningxia Region under the control of the Communist Party, only a few painters were still engaged in oil paintings. Most of the painters however adopted the more popular art forms that were suitable for political purposes, and many practiced wood engravings. The artistic and political views of Lu Xun, the realism of Xu Beihong and his belief that "sketch is the basis of all form of modeling arts" were in line with the doctrine of Mao Zedong's art theory and had become the mainstream of arts in Yan'an. Though wood engraving became the only art medium, artists in Yan'an had not stopped their artistic endeavor and accumulated large quantity of successful experience. They believed that the past traditions should serve the need of the present and the foreign arts should serve the requirement of China proposed by Mao Zedong's theory. Compared with the wood engravings in Shanghai in 1930s, their works were more fluent with nationality and were more realistic.

During the early period of new China, painters faced new topics and they had to deal with many issues of the time, the relationship between art and politics, how to serve the needs of workers, peasants and soldiers, and how to experience the lives of common people. Every painter had a task of adjustment to embrace the new era. Realist paintings with expression of idealism to depict the themes of new life in the new period were very popular among painters. Oil paintings of 1950s mainly reflected revolutionary history and the effort to build a new China. The government selected students to the former Soviet Union and East European socialist countries to learn painting and also invited painters from the Soviet Union and Romania to teach at two national fine art institutes in Beijing and Hangzhou. Chinese students not only learned oil painting skills, but also accepted the painting methods of socialist realism. Viewing from the achievements during this period, the apparent extreme art concepts and practice during the revolutionary era to art development was not all destructive, as asserted by some people. There was an urgency to reform the stagnate field of art and the lifeless scholar paintings after the "Four Wangs" had reached an end and could not continue. The new society and Chinese people, which had experienced great changes, need new visual images. Socialist realism paintings successfully adopted its new functions to promote the national interest and to depict the new life of people. Artists preferred to the optimistic and exaggerative styles of folk arts, even they used the traditional art forms. Meanwhile, it was inevitable that artists could not entirely practice without any trace of the old. Those paintings which were entitled of "revolutionary romanticism" were merely the mixture of heroism of a new era, Utopian intention and petty bourgeoisie interest. However, these paintings still had illustrated a new style of confidence, and romantic realistic, full of new and traditional national characteristics.

The overwhelming Cultural Revolution (1966–1976) pushed the new art movement to the very limit. Starting from the end of 1960s, eight newly

Before Going to the University, by Wen Chengzhi, 1970s

adopted Peking Operas with revolutionary realism themes were imposed forcedly to the society and used as models at that time not only for the drama but also all other art works were governed by the eight model operas. This directly led to appearance of many paintings similar to the stage settings and scenes of the eight model operas. In a retrospective view, paintings at that time were easily criticized as pretentious, exaggerative and extremely political. But paintings were always art, and even though the painter himself claimed that he entirely serve the politics, the artistic challenge never cease to be present. Leaving aside political elements, the paintings during the Cultural Revolution, featured with "red, glory and light," probably meant the construction of a new but powerful visual system, which required new painting skills and artistic ability to command the artistic expressions. This was an unique combination of modernism and nationalism and was socialist realism art with Chinese characteristics. This new expression could not be found either in the Chinese traditional

Chairman Mao's Trip to Anyuan, by Liu Chunhua, 1967.

paintings such as the scholar painting and folk paintings, or in the western classical and modern arts. The sincerity and courage the artists had showed in their pursuit of art during this complex period of time are admirable.

We should examine four representative works at that time to illustrate their artistic endeavor. Dong Xiwen's oil painting *Inauguration Ceremony of the People's Republic of China* (*Kaiguo Dadian*), Luo Gongliu's oil painting *Tunnel Warfare* (*Didao Zhan*), Kang Zuotian's Chinese traditional painting *Red Sun's Radiance Warms Ten Thousand of Generations* (*Hongtaiyang Guanghui Nuan Wandai*) and Chen Yanning's oil painting *Chairman Mao Inspects Rural Areas in Guangdong* (*Maozhuxi Shicha Guangdong Nongcun*). The first two were painted in 1950s while the latter two were products of 1971 during the Cultural Revolution. *Kaiguo Dadian* reproduced the scene on the Tiananmen Gate on the day when new China was founded. The painter was one of best painters in China and was also an expert on Dunhuang murals. This painting illustrated the painter's intention of combining the realistic skills of the west paintings with the flat coloring technique of Chinese artistic expression. The second painting *Tunnel Warfare* depicted the courage and wisdom of Chinese people during the war against Japanese invasion. The painter was a specialist from the era of Luxun Art School of Yan'an. The painting was a perfect merge of revolutionist determination and the western oil classic techniques. The theme of the third painting is the contrast of the past miseries and the present joys. It is a non-scholar Chinese traditional painting painted with Chinese traditional painting materials of Xuan paper, ink and colors. The figures in the painting were vigorous and bright and painter skillfully showed life-like portral of objects and the bright sunshine, symbol of the new society. *Chairman Mao Inspects Rural Areas in Guangdong*, of course, focused on Chairman Mao. But the most impressive of the painting is the image of "new socialism countryside," and especially the farmers of South China depicted. If these paintings are viewed and discussed from the perspectives of the "world

New Soldiers at the Mine, by Yang Zhiguang, early in 1970s.

Dong Xiwen, *The Founding Ceremony of the People's Republic of China* (310cm×176cm), oil painting on canvas, completed in 1953.

fine art" and the "Chinese traditional fine art", there is one obvious feature: the collective creation of Chinese painters during this particular period of history is irreplaceable. Artistic products is always a part of society to which it belongs and every single product is the carrier and symbol of the culture and social system it represents; on the other hand, every artistic product reflects the history of individual efforts and the journey of personnel development. Once the product is completed, its relationship with or relevance to the specific fact and social environment is not that important any more. Thus, the artistic values are far more treasured than its social contribution once made.

"Modern" and "Post-Modern"

In 1979, the Communist Party of China held its Third Plenary Session of the 11th Central Committee, adopted an open door policy and embarked the task of leading China to the four modernizations. China entered a new era. Chinese intellectuals and artists have experienced the most relaxed academic and artistic environments since 1949. They reflected on the past era and set their earnest eyes to the world. The delayed meeting between Chinese art and western modern art stunned the Chinese intellectuals who just experienced social tribulation and spiritual destitution. They had a strong thirst and desire for knowledge. Their eagerness for the lost time and the enthusiasm to make up for the missed contacts with the artistic developments of the world was unprecedented, reminiscent of the enthusiastic scholar painters who worshiped their predecessors.

Artistic products of the new era still carried the marks of the period just ended. Although young artists showed increasing interests to the modern arts, the familiar realism paintings still attracted the attention of the society. In particular, a group of students of the Fine Art Institute of Sichuan exhibited several paintings in early 1980s and they caused a sensation in the society. The paintings described the Cultural Revolution as a tragedy. Though the painting skills were considered even to be primitive, their efforts to model their paintings on exhibitionist style of Russian painters in the 19th century and their narrative expressions echoed the sentiments of the public. Gao Xiaohua's painting *Snow on a Certain Day* (*Mounian Mouri Xue*) reminded people of Vasili I. Surikov's painting, the Morning of the Execution of the Streltsy. Only the Russian noble has been changed to a Chinese Red Guard. Luo Zhongli attempted to paint a portrait of a common worker similar to Mao Zedong's portrait on the Tiananmen Gate. His masterpiece *Father* (*Fuqin*) achieved a great success mainly because of his innovative idea. Luo Zhongli admitted he was enlightened

Chen Danqing, Shedding Tears over the Bumper Harvest, (154cm×235cm), painted in 1976.

by the photographic realism which was popular in the United States. *Pictures of Tibet* (*Xizang Zutu*) painted by Chen Danqing of Beijing Central Academy of Fine Art received more recognitions by many colleagues in the field. Chen spent his childhood in Shanghai, the only city in China once where western influence was accessible to ordinary people. Pictures of Tibet traced the realism painting style back to France's Jean Franqois Millet (1814–1875) and Gustave Courbet's (1819–1877) age. The painter was very royal to the sketch drawings he made in Tibet without unnecessary touches and refinements which were popular to many Chinese painters.

In the following decade, innovation became a major theme. Though the western modern art almost died in 1970s and so-called openness and creativeness were no longer hot topics, China inherited the flag in the 1980s' and developed it with tremendous energy. According to art critic Gao Minglu, social background dictated the development of art and China needed an elite art in 1980s. The period had a perception that pioneering art equals to the elite art. They completed their new Long March within a short period of time. They first experimented with all the west arts of

< *Scenery on Mountains* (68.4cm×45.6cm), by Li Keran (1907-1989),1984.

Father (222cm×115cm), oil painting, by Luo Guanzhong, 1980, collected by China Art Gallery.

different schools and as a result they confidently found a style of their own. Around 1985, so-called modern art exhibitions appeared like mushroom. Every exhibition and even every artist issued their own declaration of modernism. Fortunately, the Chinese modern art experimenters around 1985 did not encounter with a society with middle class and controlled by money. They could still maintain their innocent purity of arts. The first All China Modern Art Exhibition held in 1989 in Beijing did not have the usual cynical atmosphere associated with so-called modern arts. Even artists who performed grotesquely always mentioned responsibility and destiny. They still instinctly appeared in a manner of idealist and illustrated the relationship between deconstruction and reconstruction.

To some artists' surprise, though they tried their best in the modern art movement, the symbols that highlights the modern Chinese arts and that can match both the western and ancient Chinese arts were actually created during the period of time that they were eagerly to abandon. This was supported by the Venice Biennial sponsor's trip to China in 1990. Wang Guangyi's painting depicting the mass denouncement held by workers, peasants and soldiers during the Cultural Revolution was placed together with the marks of Coca-Cola. The visual symbols of Mao Zedong era and even Mao's image itself became part of the Chinese modern art. The Italian group brought many paintings of politics back to Venice and they were first shown to the west world.

Spring South of the Yangtze River (68cm×43cm), ink and wash on paper, by Wu Guanzhong, 1987.

With the progress of China's reform and open door policy, more Chinese painters realized and have to deal with the concept of markets and their temptation.

Fang Lijun, *November 1, 2005*, oil painting on canvas, 2005.

They regrouped and readjusted themselves. In comparison to the radical artists, they compromised and they still used Chinese traditional painting mediums to create arts of present time. They realized that real Chinese modern art cannot be realized by only declarations and slogans. Most artists abandoned their previous efforts to look for inspiration from the modern movements to influence the society and instead they worked to meet the demand of the market. Their effort to look for a non-western pioneering art to create Chinese modern art is itself the continuation of the balance between the west and China, modern and tradition, and elite and popular. It is a compromise and it continues.

Zhang Xiaogang, *No. 1 Big Family*, (200cm×300cm), 2001.

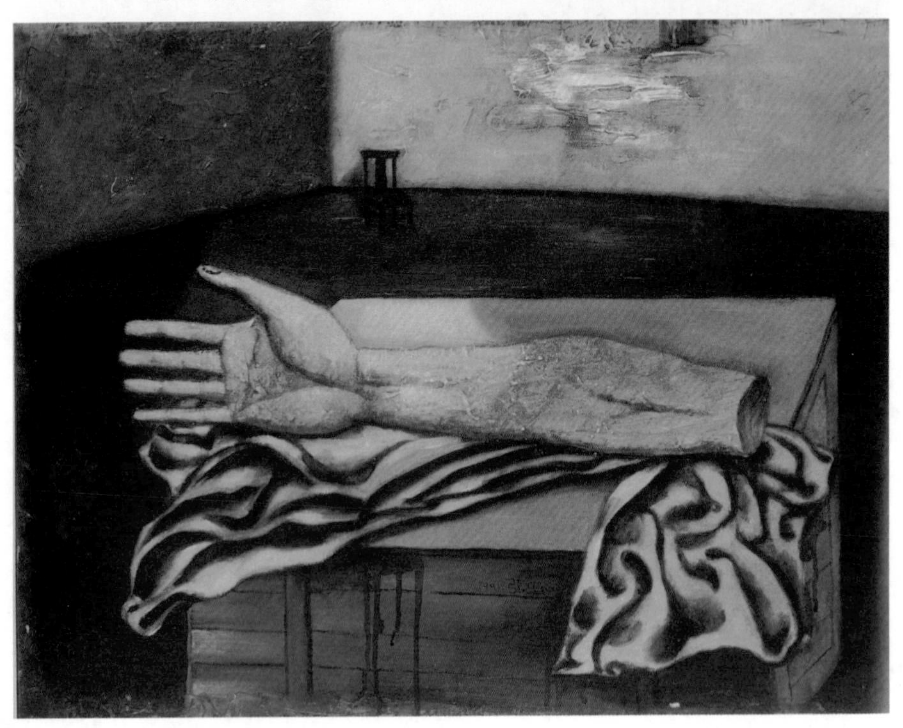

Yang Qian, *Hand*, oil painting on canvas, (50cm×70cm), 1991.

Yue Minjun, *Revolutionist*, (75cm×57cm), 2000

Liu Xiaodong, *Son*, 1995.

Appendix:
Chronological Table of the Chinese Dynasties

The Paleolithic Period	Approx. 1,700,000–10,000 years ago
The Neolithic Age	Approx. 10,000–4,000 years ago
Xia Dynasty	2070–1600 BC
Shang Dynasty	1600–1046 BC
Western Zhou Dynasty	1046–771 BC
Spring and Autumn Period	770–476 BC
Warring States Period	475–221 BC
Qin Dynasty	221–206 BC
Western Han Dynasty	206 BC–AD 25
Eastern Han Dynasty	25–220
Three Kingdoms	220–280
Western Jin Dynasty	265–317
Eastern Jin Dynasty	317–420
Northern and Southern Dynasties	420–589
Sui Dynasty	581–618
Tang Dynasty	618–907
Five Dynasties	907–960
Northern Song Dynasty	960–1127
Southern Song Dynasty	1127–1279
Yuan Dynasty	1206–1368
Ming Dynasty	1368–1644
Qing Dynasty	1616–1911
Republic of China	1912–1949
People's Republic of China	Founded in 1949